Differentiated Literacy Strategies

Differentiated Literacy Strategies

for Student Growth and Achievement
in Grades K-6

Gayle H. Gregory • Lin Kuzmich

CORWIN PRESS
A Sage Publications Company
Thousand Oaks, California

For information:

Corwin Press
A Sage Publications Company
2455 Teller Road
Thousand Oaks, California 91320
www.corwinpress.com

Sage Publications Ltd.
1 Oliver's Yard
55 City Road
London EC1Y 1SP
United Kingdom

Sage Publications India Pvt. Ltd.
B-42, Panchsheel Enclave
Post Box 4109
New Delhi 110 017 India

Printed in the United States of America

Library of Congress Cataloging-in-Publication Data

Gregory, Gayle.
Differentiated literacy strategies for student growth and achievement in grades K-6 / Gayle H. Gregory and Lin Kuzmich.
        p. cm.
Includes bibliographical references and index.
    ISBN 0-7619-8880-7 (cloth) — ISBN 0-7619-8881-5 (pbk.)
1. Language arts (Elementary) 2. Individualized instruction. 3. Multicultural education. I. Kuzmich, Lin. II. Title.
LB1576.G773 2005
372.6—dc22   2004018164

This book is printed on acid-free paper.

04 05 06 10 9 8 7 6 5 4 3 2 1

Acquisitions Editor:	Faye Zucker
Editorial Assistants:	Stacy Wagner, Gem Rabanera
Production Editor:	Diane S. Foster
Copy Editor:	Mark Newton, Publication Services, Inc.
Typesetter:	C&M Digitals (P) Ltd.
Proofreader:	Mary Meagher
Indexer:	Will Ragsdale
Cover Designer:	Tracy E. Miller
Graphic Designer:	Lisa Miller

Contents

Preface

Gayle Gregory and Lin Kuzmich have teamed together again to write a book to help teachers of literacy skills face the realities of inclusive classrooms in an atmosphere of high accountability.

High-stakes testing in literacy and other areas, and initiatives to close the achievement gap for diverse learners, impact every aspect of teaching and learning today. Teachers have so many things coming at them at once. We wanted to create a book that sorted through the research to identify the tools, curricula, and strategies that had the best chance of accelerating literacy learning for elementary students.

We hope this book helps teachers focus on the following:

- What to teach in literacy
- Which strategies help us to accelerate literacy acquisition
- How to meet the needs of diverse learners
- How to plan strategically
- How to deepen thinking
- How to think about and select strategies diagnostically

We are enthralled by the possibilities of the twenty-first century and daunted by the enormity of its challenges at the same time. How can we prepare literate students to be successful in a world about which we can only speculate and imagine? "Educators today feel both the excitement of this emerging world and the challenge of preparing young people to live productively with it" (Bruce, 2003, p. 6).

We believe that it takes more than a basic ability to read, write, speak, and listen to be successful in this century. Competency in literacy includes using the tools of the twenty-first century and learning about new ones as they are invented. Such competency also includes solving problems, thinking about the information and knowledge we encounter, and using it in a purposeful way.

The future belongs to those of our students who attain the empowering level of literacy to reinvent themselves over a lifetime. We hope this book will be a helpful guide for new and veteran teachers planning instruction in elementary grades, for principals and instructional leaders who supervise and plan for the growth of all learners, for support personnel who assist unique learners, and for all others who care about the literacy levels and future success of all students in our complex world.

Acknowledgments

We are both teachers and practitioners at heart, and we have worked with other teachers and with students over the years in a variety of roles and grade levels. We would like to acknowledge all those other talented and committed educators who have challenged our thinking and helped clarify our ideas based on sound research and practice.

We have been enlightened and influenced by great thinkers, including Howard Gardner, Robert Sternberg, Daniel Goleman, Art Costa, Bob Garmstom, Pat Wolfe, Robert Sylwester, Barbara Givens, David Sousa, Tony Gregorc, Carol Rolheiser, Bob Marzano, Jay McTighe, Carol Ann Tomlinson, Pam Robbins, Heidi Hayes Jacob, Grant Wiggins, Richard Stiggins, Doug Reeves, Willard Daggett, Linda Elder, and Richard Paul.

We also extend our gratitude to our husbands, Joe and Steve, and our children for their patience and understanding of the time this venture took from "family hour." We could not accomplish anything worthwhile without their love and support.

It is our hope and desire that this book will be a helpful, insightful addition to the libraries of teachers, administrators, and other educators and an integral part of their planning and thinking as they design learning for all children so that all may learn and reach their potential.

—Gayle H. Gregory & Lin Kuzmich

Corwin Press and the authors extend their thanks to the following reviewers for their contributions to this volume:

Nancy Creech, Dort Elementary School, Roseville, MI

William Fitzhugh, Reisterstown Elementary School, Reisterstown, MD

Ann Fulk, Educational Consultant, Fairfax Station, VA

Steve Hutton, Elementary School Principal, Villa Hills, KY

Maria Elena Reyes, University of Alaska, Fairbanks, AK

Debbie Wilks, Riverside Cultural Arts and History Magnet School, Wichita, KS

About the Authors

Gayle H. Gregory has been a teacher in elementary, middle, and secondary schools. For many years, she taught in schools with extended periods of instructional time (block schedules). She has had extensive districtwide experience as a curriculum consultant and staff development coordinator. Most recently, she was course director at York University for the Faculty of Education, teaching in the teacher education program. She now consults internationally (Europe, Asia, North and South America, Australia) with teachers, administrators, and staff developers in the areas of managing change, differentiated instruction, brain-compatible learning, block scheduling, emotional intelligence, instructional and assessment practices, cooperative group learning, presentation skills, renewal of secondary schools, enhancing teacher quality, and coaching and mentoring.

Gayle is affiliated with many organizations, including the Association for Supervision and Curriculum Development and the National Staff Development Council. She is the author of *Differentiated Instructional Strategies in Practice: Training, Implementation, and Supervision* and the coauthor of *Designing Brain-Compatible Learning; Thinking Inside the Block Schedule: Strategies for Teaching in Extended Periods of Time; Differentiated Instructional Stategies: One Size Doesn't Fit All; Data Driven Differentiation in the Standards-Based Classroom;* and *Differentiated Literacy Strategies for Student Growth and Achievement in Grades 7–12.* She has been featured in Video Journal of Education's best-selling elementary and secondary videos, *Differentiating Instruction to Meet the Needs of All Learners.*

Gayle is committed to lifelong learning and professional growth for herself and others. She may be contacted by e-mail at gregorygayle@ netscape.net. Her Web site is www3.sympatico.ca/gayle.gregory.

 **Lin Kuzmich** is the Assistant Superintendent for Thompson School District in Loveland, Colorado, where she has also served as Executive Director of Instruction, as Director of Professional Development, and for nine years as a Principal. Before joining the Loveland District, Lin was a classroom teacher. She taught special education and reading PreK–12, high school reading, middle school language arts, and she was also an elementary school classroom teacher, earning the Teacher of the Year Award for Denver Public Schools in 1979.

For the past ten years, Lin has been involved in professional development, teaching classes at several universities, providing training for agencies and school districts throughout the United States, and authoring journal articles for government and regional publications. Her recent work has focused on data-driven instruction, standards-based education, supervision and evaluation of teachers, and data-driven school improvement planning. She is also the coauthor with Gayle Gregory of *Differentiated Literacy Strategies for Student Growth and Achievement in Grades 7–12* and *Data Driven Differentiation in the Standards-Based Classroom*. Lin works extensively with administrators and teacher leaders who want to create environments for student achievement and growth. She may be reached via e-mail at kuzenergy@comcast.net.

Introduction

MULTIPLE COMPETENCIES IN LITERACY

Twenty-first century literacy requires more from our students than a basic ability to read, write, speak, and listen. According to the landmark SCANS report (U.S. Secretary of Labor, 1991), there are five competencies that twenty-first century workers must learn from their schools:

1. Identification, organization, planning, and allocation of resources.

2. Working with others.

3. Acquiring and using information.

4. Understanding complex interrelationships.

5. Working with a variety of technologies.

Thus basic reading skills are no longer enough. Learners must achieve multiple competencies that will allow them to become creative, adept, and competently literate adults.

Literacy learning starts in the earliest grades. What we teach, and what we choose to teach with, matters in the creation of the complex, lifelong learning patterns needed in this century. Competency in literacy involves solving problems, thinking about the information and knowledge we encounter, and then using it in purposeful ways.

To attain empowering levels of literacy that align with the SCANS competencies, young learners need to accelerate their growth in at least four different domains of literacy:

- Functional literacy
- Content area literacy
- Technological literacy
- Innovative or creative literacy

This book brings together the research, tools, curricula, and strategies that will give today's teachers the best chance of helping the diverse learners in their classrooms to accelerate growth and achievement in all four literacies.

The book is organized in sections. Chapter 1 is an introduction to the four literacies and will help us frame our concept of meeting diverse learner needs. Chapters 2 and 3 are about classroom climate and knowing how diverse learners learn. Chapters 4 through 7 address each of the four literacies in turn and contain information and tools for curriculum, assessing what we have taught, and strategies for learning. Chapter 8 puts it all together with sample units, strategies for managing differentiated classrooms, and ideas for dealing with problems related to literacy development.

There are questions we want to answer in each chapter:

Chapter 1: What types of literacy do we need to consider to prepare diverse learners for the future?

Chapter 2: How do we create an atmosphere that sustains and supports the learning of literacy skills?

Chapter 3: What do we need to know about our learners, and how will we gather and use that information?

Chapter 4: What are the basics that every literate person needs to know, and how do our young learners acquire the initial skills of functional literacy?

Chapter 5: How can we better access and utilize *content-area* skills and information?

Chapter 6: How can we use literacy skills in technological and multimedia venues to create products and demonstrations of learning?

Chapter 7: How can we use literacy skills to solve complex problems and produce *innovative* concepts and products?

Chapter 8: How can teachers manage the variety of configurations in our differentiated classrooms, close learning gaps, and focus on growth and achievement for all of our students?

Table 0.1 offers an outline of the various elements in this book to facilitate mixing and matching strategies within and across chapters.

Meeting diverse learner needs is also well-served by integrating these literacies with proven methods of differentiated learning. Differentiation offers us powerful ways to focus our curriculum so that we may begin to address the high stakes for the future success of our students. In the words of Carl Sagan, "Both skepticism and wonder are skills that need honing and practice. Their harmonious marriage within the mind of every school child ought to be a principal goal of public education" (Sagan, 1996, p. 306).

Robert Sternberg (1996) maintains that, "Children with other kinds of abilities may be derailed from the fast track early in life, with the result that they never get the opportunity to show what they really can do" (p. 202). We need to make certain that we are preparing students for the future and not leaving some students on a slower or less productive track. Our expectations around literacy will shape the speed at which we can close the gap with some learners and ensure the growth of all learners. Accepting less will create an unthinkable future for our students.

Table 0.1   Differentiated literacy strategies for Grades K–6

Creating a Climate for Literacy	Knowing the Learner	Functional Literacy	Content Area Literacy	Technological Literacy	Innovative Literacy	Managing the Literacy Classroom
Building Connections Risk taking Resilience Perseverance Appreciating diversity **What to Avoid** Fear Humiliation Disconnection **Foster and Sustain Growth** Feedback Reflective Learning Rituals Respect Cultural history Celebration **Creating Positive Conditions for Literacy** Reading Writing Speaking Listening	**Brain Research** Principles and implications **Best Practices** Marzano's 9 **Developmental Stages for Ages 5 through 12** Reading Writing **Status of Reader and Writer** Emerging Developing Fluent **Learning Styles** Preferences Needs **Multiple Intelligences** Brain functioning Literacy connections **Choice Boards**	**Oral Language** Phonics Spelling Comprehension Fluency **Funny Thing About English** **Grouping** T.A.P.S. Total group Alone Pairs Small group **Balanced Reading** Read-Alouds Buddy Shared Guided Literature circles Round-robin reading groups **Writing** Narrative Descriptive **Choice Boards**	**Vocabulary** **Concept Development** **Text Orientation** Before During After reading K.W.L. Anticipation guide Highlighting Note taking Summarizing Sticky notes SQ3R Reciprocal Paper pass Split page Advanced organizers Graphics **Writing** Expository Persuasive **Choice Boards**	**Information Literacy** Definition Locating Select and analyze Organize and synthesize Create and present Evaluating **Questioning** Clarity Assumptions Bias **Searching for Information** **Production Planning Guides** Audience Purpose Graphics Solution focus Self-evaluation **Diverse Learners** Demystifying directions Spatial factor Spelling factor	**Innovative Literacy and Creativity** Student question formation Elaboration Generalization Creativity square R.A.F.T. Choice board **Workplace Skills** **Prose, Document and Quantitative Literacy** Selecting materials **Scenario-Based Learning** Loading the shopping cart The dragon is sleeping **Influence and Ethics** Writing Speaking Listening	**Unit Planning Across Literacies** **Managing Diverse Classrooms** **Learners With Literacy Problems** **Centers** Sample centers Organizing ideas Assigning centers Tracking Agendas **Challenging Writers and Readers** **Developing Independent Learners** Contracts Focus and sponge activities

Accelerating Literacy Learning

1

"Let us put our minds together and see what life we can make for our children."

—Chief Sitting Bull (1877)

ACADEMIC ACCOUNTABILITY

In the dark ages, when we started teaching, we were not held accountable for much of anything related to student growth and achievement. Dialogue with the principal went something like this:

> Your students are sitting in their chairs and raising their hands. It is good that your lesson plans are ready for the substitute. Have you thought about the new deadline for getting your grades into the office?

Then we began to focus on the expectation that teachers would follow a process when instructing. The dialogue with the principal then went something like this:

Your wait time is good, and the ideas for initially engaging students at the start of the lesson seem to be working. You may want to write out two or three questions ahead of time to check for understanding.

But the 1990s brought us standards-based education, and the focus for accountability became student learning. The dialogue with the principal in many schools now goes something like this:

If I walk through your classroom, will the students know what standard you are teaching? I like the performance assessment you created for that unit.

But, given the proper excuses about home life, disability, or language limitations, we still don't always mean real accountability for all students. The twenty-first century accountability challenge, however, says that we will not leave students behind and, more significantly, that we will close the learning gap for all groups of students.

CLOSING THE ACHIEVEMENT GAP

The first thing that many teaching texts tell us about the achievement gap is to quit making excuses and get on with it. That is a worthy mission, but it is harder than it looks. We have outstanding educators working hard in classrooms and schools all over the country. These are dedicated and innovative people. We have research that tells us about powerful and exciting strategies that work, but we still need to know where to start and which tools and strategies to employ for which students. Knowing when to utilize these top-notch strategies would be helpful information as well.

This means the teacher-principal dialogue needs to shift to a discussion of what incremental growth looks like for each group of students and to careful consideration of how we articulate the curriculum through the expected level of student work and performance. The principal may need to join a lesson study group or a group of teachers who are using student work for evaluation and lesson planning. That could provide one of the best venues for effective dialogue that focuses on the academic growth of every student.

So what does our retrospective look at the recent history of education have to do with this book? We believe that the key to closing the achievement gap for any individual student or group of students lies in the acquisition of skills and demonstrations of learning that clearly reflect a high degree of literacy. Without a focus on literacy, it is hard to imagine the acceleration of learning needed to demonstrate increased scores on high-stakes tests, let alone other worthy accomplishments appropriate for success in the twenty-first century.

DIVERSE LEARNERS AND BUSY TEACHERS

In the United States and in many other countries, teachers are currently held accountable for closing the learning gap for all racial and ethnic groups; students identified as disabled; gender groups; students living in poverty; students for whom English is not the primary language; and, in some states, regions, or districts, for students who may be identified as gifted or talented. In this book, we want to highlight literacy strategies that are likely to be useful with many different kinds of learners, but, in addition to *useful,* we've added an additional criterion: We also want to focus on literacy strategies that show promise for *increasing student success* and, in some cases, increasing such success *rapidly.*

We believe that is the way to help teachers make gap-closing choices. Teachers do not work the way of doctors and lawyers. We don't meet with most students one-on-one, and we don't have a team of folks to back us up by assisting with paperwork or running diagnostic tests. We are teachers in classrooms working with multiple and diverse students, or we are specialists, administrators, and leaders working to support multiple and diverse teachers and students in multiple and diverse classroom settings.

We need practical strategies that address the realities of classroom conditions. Those realities include issues such as the following:

- What do I do with twenty-four students while I do a miscue analysis or individual reading inventory with one student?
- I have seven students with Individualized Education Plans (IEPs), and each one is unique.
- I have five students from three countries: Some speak a little English, and the two who arrived last week speak no English.
- I have twelve students who scored below proficient on the state reading and writing assessment and three who scored advanced.
- Which of my students ate a meal today, and which of them have a home to go to this evening?

We could add another twenty-five modifiers to describe many urban and rural classrooms in our schools today. That means our goal must be to provide teachers with the right strategies for the right students when time, resources, and support are limited.

SELECTING HIGH-PAYOFF INSTRUCTIONAL STRATEGIES

In this book we have used icons and descriptors to organize and differentiate learning and teaching strategies and to indicate their value or payoff for a particular type of learner. They are all great strategies for any teacher's repertoire, but our particular goal here is to help busy teachers meet diverse learner needs in every lesson and every unit.

We also need to think about how to frame the questions regarding the systematic and productive instruction of various types of learners. This will yield better strategy selections for teachers and a higher payoff for students. For example, instead of asking how to manage special education students in general education classrooms, we can get more specific. We can ask the following questions:

- How do we accommodate and advance the growth of students who have learning disabilities as well as linguistic difficulties?
- Which strategies are most useful for primary grade males who struggle with narrative writing?
- How do we handle a learner who knows a little English, but not enough to speak fluently?

This book will help you to formulate those questions and then provide you with some of the strategies shown by research to provide the most promise for student growth for the relevant individuals and learner subgroups. When discussing learner subgroups it is not functional for a teacher to speak only of a student on an IEP. A teacher needs to know the type of disability and the expectations for accommodations to select strategies that meet a particular student's needs. What if that same child is twice exceptional, perhaps gifted in specific academic areas such as mathematics and science? Then identifying learner needs and selecting instructional strategies may become extraordinarily complex (see Table 1.1).

The extraordinary variety within learner subgroups is why Marzano, Pickering, and Pollack's (2001) nine strategies and Gardner's (1983) multiple intelligences are so attractive to teachers. It is easier for teachers to think about a small group of top-notch strategies than a hundred strategies of undetermined usefulness. But we would like to introduce another option as well: Teachers can learn a repertoire of top-notch instructional strategies that also meet specific types of learner needs.

For example, we could choose to discuss buddy reading rather than round-robin reading. We know that buddy reading increases fluency, benefits young learners, reduces risk factors for English Language Learners, and helps males who are reluctant readers. But we also know that buddy reading may not be the best strategy for special needs learners

Table 1.1   Variation within student subgroups

Subgroup							
Special Education	Linguistic Disability	Content Area—Specific Processing Difficulty	Physical	Emotional	Cognitive Disability	Other: Autism, Multi-categorical	
English Language Learner	No English	Survival Personal and Social English	Survival Content Area English	Functional Personal and Social English	Functional Content Area English	Competent Personal and Social English	Competent Content Area English
Poverty	Homeless	Generational Poverty	Temporary or Situational Poverty				
Gender	Male	Female					
Gifted	General Giftedness	Specific Area Giftedness	Specific Area Talented				
Ethnic	Cultural Influences	Racial Influences	Geographic Influences				

5

Table 1.2   Sample strategy format

Strategy: *Buddy Reading*

Literacy Competency: Functional Literacy for Reading Fluency

Description: In Buddy Reading students take turns reading to each other to increase fluency

Advantages: Increases the amount of reading aloud, allows external looping (hearing the words for imprint in the brain), takes advantage of students' natural inclination for social interaction, and is less emotionally risky than reading aloud to the class or in a small group

How to Use: Pair students who are less able with those who are more able readers. Choose text that is at the learning level, not the frustrating level. Can be paired with a graphic organizer to address comprehension of reading selection. Adjust time for activity by age level appropriateness. Students trade off oral reading to each other by paragraph, page, or section of the selection.

Source: (Tompkins, 2003)

Bottom Line Examples:

⇑ This strategy works well for young learners who need to increase their fluency, it reduces the risk factor for English Language Learners, and it helps males who are reluctant readers

⇓ This strategy does not work as well for special education learners with linguistic or auditory processing difficulties or for an advanced reader who is already fluent. However it may work with additional modifications

---

with linguistic processing difficulties or advanced readers who are already fluent. The bottom line in this book is that we will give you those indicators for the well-researched strategies we propose, identifying which types of learners may benefit from each strategy and which learners may not be as well-served (see Table 1.2).

STANDARDS-BASED CURRICULUM

What should teachers teach and what should students learn are critical questions. We have only so much time, and, even with standards-based education, we cannot do it all well. In reading, writing, speaking, and listening, we still need to decide where to focus our attention and how to divide our time. Not all standards and grade-level benchmarks or indicators are created equal. Doug Reeves (2000) and Larry Ainsworth (2003) are among those who talk about "power standards," those standards that are the most critical and on which we should focus much of our time. For literacy, most state standards commonly look like this:

"Students will read and write for a variety of purposes and audiences." Entire courses and curricula across grade levels could be written to define that standard. So many different instructional materials and approaches could work that it is difficult to rule out those that might not fit.

Deciding what is important to teach and, for which learners such things should be taught remains challenging. Often, state, county, or district departments of education define discrete skills for each grade level that must be mastered for the state assessment, and, although these definitions may help a teacher plan time, they do not help students learn. So we must add a framework that makes sense in diverse classrooms. We must plan ahead for students if they are to be lifelong, literate learners in the twenty-first century.

FOUR CORE COMPETENCIES IN LITERACY

We cannot focus our literacy efforts on just early reading. We do regard and define a level of functional literacy as essential. Foundational use of phonics, demonstration of fluency, oral language use, early writing, and initial meaning creation are critical aspects of functional literacy, but our twenty-first century learners need more than a functional literacy basis to plan for a future that will include new careers and technologies we cannot even imagine. Complex international influences, changing and emerging employment situations, and interpersonal and social conditions all require us to read, write, speak, and listen for a variety of purposes and then to take actions based on that understanding. "Instruction in metacognitive strategies can improve reading comprehension. Good comprehenders read to purpose and actively monitor their own understanding of what they read" (RAND Report, 2002).

In this book we look at four major competencies in literacy that help us weave student learning strategies into the future:

1. Functional Literacy

2. Content Area Literacy

3. Technological Literacy

4. Innovative Literacy

What do we need to know about these literacies, and how will they help us close the learning gap for diverse students? Table 1.3 and Figure 1.1 offer definitions and explanations of how these literacies can work together to help our students survive and thrive in the twenty-first century.

Table 1.3   Factors critical to development of the four types of literacy

TYPE OF LITERACY	CRITICAL FACTORS
1. Functional Literacy	
Defined as: Learning to read, write, speak, and listen **Purpose:** To teach students how to read and write to a basic level of functioning by the end of third grade or, for those just learning English, by the third to fifth year of learning the language **Sources:** McEwan, (2002); U.S. Department of Health and Human Services (2000) *"[T]hey will need to acquire an intimate knowledge of the code: the conventionally accepted way in which letters or groups of letters correspond to spoken sounds in our language"* (McEwan, 2002, p. 32).	***Oral Language Development:*** Including speaking and listening ***Phonological Awareness:*** Sounds and their differences ***Phonemics:*** Translating sounds into symbols, learning the symbols ***Spelling/Early Writing:*** Translating symbols into and words in writing to convey meaning ***Fluency:*** Rate of reading, flow of sounds, without the interference of errors ***Creating Meaning:*** Constructing what the written words are about, main ideas, literal information, details noted from words, pictures, speech, and other sources, easily getting the "gist" of a passage of print or graphic ***Narrative Writing and Descriptive:*** Telling a story, making comparisons, detailed descriptions, other forms of creative writing
2. Content Area Literacy	
Defined as: Reading, writing, speaking, and listening to demonstrate content area learning **Purpose:** Understanding and use of content area-specific knowledge and skills directed toward a specific result or demonstration of skill through a variety of means **Sources:** Vacca and Vacca (2002), Harvey and Goudvis (1998, 2000), Miller (2003), Burke (2000), Benjamin (2002) *Academic literacy differs from the literacy that is required to read fiction. When we read fiction, we usually do so for pleasure, looking to lose ourselves in the beauty of the language and the story. With academic readings, we need to employ strategies of reading that are directed more toward finding specific information and remembering it* (Benjamin, 2002, p. 29).	***Vocabulary Acquisition:*** Gateway to using content area knowledge, development and interconnection of concepts in a content area ***Questioning:*** Formulating questions to understand and inquire further about a content area skill or concept ***Text Orientation:*** Understanding the construction and factors that aid meaning in text or material construction for a particular content area including graphical or visual representations as well as book parts and text clues ***Expository Writing:*** Factual information to recount or inform or direct a reader. Convey thinking about a content area topic or problem, note patterns or trends, and demonstrate usefulness of the content area ***Presentation and Product Creation:*** Performance-based summative demonstration of the integration of information and skills given a topic or problem

TYPE OF LITERACY	CRITICAL FACTORS
3. Technological Literacy	
Defined as: Using reading, writing, speaking, and listening in multimedia venues to create products and demonstrations of learning **Purpose:** Multidimensional thinking and production through access, use, and creation employing technology-based tools and strategies. **Sources:** Thornburg (1991), Bruce (2003) *"As a user of personal computers, you can help others understand the benefit of this technology in extending students' ability to explore the space of concepts and ideas"* (Thornburg, 1991, p. 13).	***Questioning Authenticity:*** Applying criteria to establish author and Web site credibility, detecting assumptions, purpose, and clarity ***Searching for Information:*** Utilizing the nature and structure of Web-based information to find what you need, demonstrate dimensional or embedded thinking and solve problems ***Media Orientation:*** What is the best method for the product and meaning you must convey or produce ***Production:*** Utilizing computer-based and other multimedia production to demonstrate literacy competencies and produce products to convey meaning, solutions, and adaptations ***Demystifying Directions:*** Understanding and using directions in multiple forms and verbal or written construction of sequential steps for use of technological and other tools and processes
4. Innovative Literacy	
Defined as: Reading, writing, speaking, and listening to do or solve something complex, invent something unique, or produce something innovative **Purpose:** Develop the adaptability and orientation to work and life inside and outside of the school setting to survive and thrive amid rapid change and expansion of knowledge **Sources:** Sternberg (1996); Manzo (1998); Manzo, Barnhill, Land, Manzo, and Thomas (1997); Manzo, Manzo, and Albee (2002); Manzo, Manzo, Barnhill, and Thomas (2000); Manzo, Manzo, and Estes (2001); Barton (2003) *Successfully intelligent people are flexible in adapting to the roles they need to fulfill. They recognize that they will have to change the way they work to fit the task and situation at hand, and then they analyze what these changes will have to be and make them* (Sternberg, 1996, p.153).	***Innovation and Creativity:*** Entrepreneurial sense of thinking and acting, fluid and flexible in use of information and transformation of knowledge into new things, attitudes, solutions, products, and/or actions ***Lifelong Learner Orientation:*** Acquiring marketable skills over time, responding to anticipated need, and creating ways to assimilate and accommodate to change, regardless of speed of the change ***Practical and Adaptive Thinking:*** Scenario-based thinking and responses to real-life situations, interpreting new information, inquiry, consumer skills that are self-selected based on desired result. Adapting the information or interactions to make decisions or plans for the present and the future ***Influential Communication:*** Communicating to convince others of a point of view, applying rationale, ethical, and congruent logic that supports creative, positive solutions and conclusions

Figure 1.1   Four types of literacy critical to the future success of our students

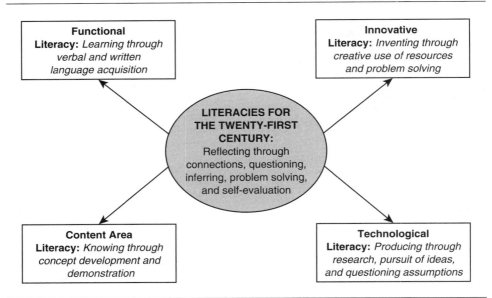

Standards and Curriculum

The four literacies act as a lens for the standards and curriculum for which teachers are accountable, and they can help us frame the critical elements for which we want to hold students accountable. Each of the four literacies is critical to the overall development of our students and their ability to access and process information at an accelerating rate in an ever-changing world. Although each one can be taught separately, most learning will lend itself to a combination of literacies. This will help us select key standards-based concepts and strategies that help students focus on skills to demonstrate content learned in many ways.

Critical Thinking

Across each of the literacies is embedded the idea of critical thinking:

- **Schema development:** summarizing and generalizing concepts and ideas, making connections from the known to the unknown
- **Inferential thinking:** discovering the meaning behind the obvious; using cause and effect analysis; determining point of view, voice, and congruence in thinking

- **Questioning:** formulating questions that determine assumptions, allow self-evaluation, and establish purpose and clarity
- **Problem solving:** analyzing a problem and developing solutions that make sense, then speaking, writing, or producing to convey solutions and methods

Instructional Strategies

Which instructional strategies have the highest payoff? Marzano, Pickering, and Pollack (2001) looked at the research carefully and did a metacognitive study of strategies that resulted in increased performance for students. Table 1.4 summarizes the literacy tactics shown to have resulted in percentile gains when used to teach thinking, reflecting, and literacy skills that connect to what we know about the brain. We will refer to and use these and other research-based instructional strategies throughout this book. We will also look at each of the four literacies in more detail and then show you the natural connections and advantages in planning units for various grade levels and subjects.

ASSESSMENT DATA

We will highlight numerous strategies in this book that work equally well for gathering both formal and informal data, instructing, and demonstrating learning. Data-driven decisions are critically important to choosing the most valuable instructional strategies for diverse learners in a variety of circumstances. This type of thinking will help us make the numerous adjustments that diverse student growth requires (Gregory & Kuzmich, 2004).

Painless Diagnostic Assessment for Young Students

In a Colorado school, two first-grade teachers have developed and planned a two-week unit on nursery rhymes and Mother Goose for the start of the school year. The entire unit will be a preassessment of their students' literacy skills. During those two weeks, the students will do the following:

- Listen and recite rhymes
- Write and draw about the rhymes
- Use a computer program that does interactive reading and play
- Read their favorite rhymes
- Read new and unfamiliar rhymes
- Create their own new rhyme or tale

(Text continued on page 14)

Table 1.4 Research-based literacy tactics and percentile gains in student performance

Strategy	%ile Gain	Connections to Brain Research	Literacy Tactics
Using similarities and differences, analogies, and metaphors	45	The brain is a pattern-seeking device. It naturally looks for connections and relationships between and among prior and new learning.	• Classifying • Compare contrast • Venn Diagrams • Synectics • Concept attainment • Concept formation
Summarizing and note taking	34	Relevance and meaning are important to the brain. It deletes what is not useful.	• Mind maps • Concept webs • Jigsaw activities • Reciprocal • Templates and advance organizers
Reinforcing effort and providing recognition	29	The brain responds positively to challenge and negatively to threat. Emotions enhance or negate learning.	• Goal setting and feedback or reflection • Journals • Portfolios
Assigning homework and practice	28	Practice and rehearsal is necessary to put new information into long-term memory. Marzano et al. (2001) suggest that learners need 24 practice trials to reach 80 percent mastery.	• Extension of application • Four squares • Book bags • Puppets • Five-finger writing
Generating nonlinguistic representations	27	The brain is a parallel processor. Visual stimuli are recalled with 90% accuracy.	• Mind maps • Graphic organizers • Models
Using cooperative learning	27	The brain is social and desires opportunities to process and make meaning through interaction and dialogue.	• Shared reading • Guided reading • Reciprocal learning • Peer editing • Buddy reading • Choral reading • Progressive writing • Jigsaw activities • Literature circles

Strategy	%ile Gain	Connections to Brain Research	Literacy Tactics
Setting objectives and providing feedback	23	Relaxed alertness is important for the brain. High challenge and low threat are optimal for learners. The brain likes to have purpose and know where the learner is going. This provides safety, clarity, and structure.	• Goal setting • Rubrics • Clear criteria • High expectations • Appropriate challenge and choice
Generating and testing hypothesis	23	The brain is curious and seeks meaning and clarity. It establishes schemas for future use and makes meaning through patterns.	• Research papers • Investigations • Debates • Persuasive writing
Providing questions, cues, and advance organizers.	22	The brain appreciates wholes and parts. The brain has to have schemas and mental constructs on which to hook new learning.	• Levels of Bloom's taxonomy • Paul and Elder's standards for questions • Agenda maps • Guided reading • Diagrams and charts • Graphic organizers • Templates and advance organizers

Source: Adapted with permission from Parry and Gregory (2003).

Note: For a fuller discussion of this topic, see Marzano, Norford, Paynter, Gaddy, and Pickering (2001).

Preassessment activities will continue in other areas as well:

- In physical education, the teacher will ask the students to act out the actions of the characters from rhymes
- In art, students will create and illustrate books and finger puppets
- In music, students will sing familiar tunes

What kinds of data will teachers have when the unit is complete? Will it help them plan for future instruction and learning? Teachers will know about the following and more:

- Phonological awareness
- Application of phonemic strategies
- Fluency
- Sense of meaning and thinking
- Sense of purpose
- Fine and gross motor skills
- Sense of linguistics
- Oral language
- Semantic acquisition strategies
- Social interaction skills
- Technology skills
- Creativity
- Initiation and problem solving
- Group cooperation

What a high-payoff process! Clearly, one effective way to preassess literacy skills is through the use of an initial engaging unit of study that integrates many areas of literacy.

Ongoing Formative Assessment

Not all assessments need to be individual or formally written and recorded. The collection of the right kind of informal data can be invaluable in helping teachers plot out next steps. From a unit like this, a teacher can flexibly group students for phonics, select (and help a student select) materials of an appropriate level to advance fluency and meaning, choose the next steps in writing and fine motor coordination, plan the type of sharing needed to advance oral language skills, and much more.

Diagnostic thinking is an essential element in a successful literacy program that meets and accelerates the learning of diverse students. In many classrooms, we have data about student learning, and teachers have a repertoire of strategies to help students learn. We must connect what we learn about student performance with our selection of strategies. We will accelerate learning if we choose strategies that make sense given current student demonstrations of literacy. This is an ongoing process. We must collect classroom data frequently so that we can adjust our strategies to reflect student speed of learning and success with learning (see Table 1.5). Waiting three months to discover that a student did not make the expected progress won't work to close a learning gap. Continuous strategy adjustment and monitoring will increase the accuracy of our instruction and thereby increase the probability that students will demonstrate growth in literacy skills.

Table 1.5   Selected methods for collecting assessment data about literacy skills

Type of Literacy	Selected Data Collection Methods
Functional Literacy	Oral reading for fluency Writing sample Verbal report, description, or story Retell a written or oral story Write a question or two with the answer Identify the main idea Miscue analysis (noting phonological and phonemic errors) Draw a picture to represent an idea or story Create a word list for writing Correct a writing sample to conventional spelling, grammar, punctuation, or capitalization Narrative or descriptive writing that tells a story, makes comparisons, gives details, and is creative
Content Area Literacy	Graphic organizer completion Note taking Homework Develop questions for investigation of a topic or issue Choose a topic or problem to investigate Expository writing samples, both short and long Presentation of a project or solution Explanation of a process or solution Interpretation of a visual or graphic piece of information Correct a writing sample for word choice accuracy and variety Create a written or verbal summary Cause and effect analysis Analyze a problem and develop solutions Write to test a premise, determine a point of view, express voice, report, or draw conclusions Correct a writing sample for voice, details, evidence, and conclusions Predict outcomes or effects Generalize concepts through application-oriented activities like role plays or simulations

(Continued)

Table 1.5 (Continued)

Type of Literacy	Selected Data Collection Methods
Technological Literacy	Scavenger hunt for sources on the Internet Question an assumption Self-evaluate work Create a flowchart for a search or information Map a complex idea Choose the best product or resources for the desired results Computer-generated writing samples Graphic organizer generation or other visual representation like Microsoft PowerPoint or drawing programs Generate directions or implement action based on complex directions Teach others a process, program, or product using various media Correct a writing sample for format, graphics, color, and other media
Innovative Literacy	Use a "4 Squares for Creativity" organizer Anticipate a need or develop a solution to a possible problem Create budget, graph data based on self-generated data Respond to a scenario, participate in a simulation Self-select method of learning and justify the choice Persuasive writing sample Detect errors and describe how to fix them Generate multiple and creative uses for an object Anticipate the needs of self and others in completing a complex task, listing necessary resources or assistance Correct a writing sample for innovative ideas, point of view, adequacy of a claim and evidence to back it up, creativity of conclusions

A COMPREHENSIVE LITERACY PROGRAM

Comprehensive literacy instruction should include the four literacies in two distinct ways. First, strengthening these areas of literacy gives us tools and support for the traditional literacy skills of reading, writing, speaking, and listening, but also important for learners are the emerging literacy skills that will support successful lifelong learning in the twenty-first century.

In the first example, technology can be a tool that helps learners with special needs who struggle with fluidity in writing. It can provide a more effective means of getting thoughts down than handwritten work would allow. In the second arena, learning to search for information in a

Web-based environment is a distinct form of literacy that is recent and evolving. An enterprising, real-life project may engage an otherwise reluctant second-grade male student in ways that haven't engaged him before. Added payoff comes as adaptive reasoning; using multiple sources of information becomes an essential and highly valued literacy skill in the work world.

This type of approach goes beyond deep thinking and higher order skills to the combination of information assimilation, creative use of products or process, and a transformative goal such as the invention of a product or creation of a Web-based business. In this book we will apply these literacies to the growth of diverse learners and identify tools to assist struggling, functional, and advanced learners.

Creating a 2
Climate for
Literacy
Learning

"To control and sort young people for the sake of institutional efficiency is to crush the human spirit."

—Ron Miller (1990, Introduction)

EQUITY, DIVERSITY, AND CLASSROOM CLIMATE

When we started outlining this book, we wanted to create a toolkit that would help educators increase literacy in students across various populations and needs. We hoped that a focus on closing the achievement gap would be meaningful to teachers struggling in an era of high-stakes assessments and yearly progress accountability.

What we learned as we reviewed the research and interviewed children, parents, administrators, teachers, and literacy coaches was that closing the achievement gap is not as simple as providing high-quality instruction using a few research-based strategies applied equally to all students. We also learned that we needed to take a serious look at what to encourage and what to avoid.

Teaching and working with diverse populations is effective only when we steer clear of stereotypes and assumptions that may or may not be correct. In planning for successful learning, we need to account for diversity, avoid equity traps, and actively seek out and use bias-reducing tools (see Table 2.1). Those are good first steps toward creating the right classroom climate for literacy learning. Students cannot be successful learners without feeling a connection to the culture, climate, and people of a school.

Table 2.1   Classrooms that respect the richness of diversity

Equity Traps	Bias-Reducing Tools & Attitudes
Exclusionary Language	**Inclusive Language**
Boys like . . . All Spanish speakers . . . All disabled students have trouble writing Asians show respect by . . . Gifted learners have pushy parents	Many students like . . . These words are similar in Spanish . . . Cultural contributions to our language . . . Understanding language acquisition and strategies that support students Asking clarifying questions Relationships are key
Assumptions About Groups	**Questions About Students**
Assuming characteristics about groups Special education students will only reach a lower level of skill demonstration with the standards	Appreciating differences, having high expectations Given the right tools, special education students will be able to demonstrate the higher expectations required in the standards-based classroom
Isolating Climate	**Engaging Climate**
Allowing students to hide in your classroom At least they are quiet These students can learn by listening "If you finish early, please help . . ." All I know is that she has never had a referral to the office If they want to go out for sports or clubs, they just need to sign up	Strategies that invite and insist upon participation such as T.A.P.S. and Think-Pair-Share Reinforce for risk-taking and celebrate the courage of participation "Select a partner to help you think out loud about the quality of your work." Students who can identify their role in class, giving students a sense of value and connection Providing support that students need to reach higher levels of performance and participation

Equity Traps	Bias-Reducing Tools & Attitudes
Dated Information	**High-Payoff Strategies**
Assuming your prior knowledge about groups of students is correct Accepting popular views without question Using a limited variety of instructional and learning strategies Believing there is one right way to teach entire groups of students	Selecting strategies with research validation Check out what is really true for particular students Question the research Conduct your own research How do I tap into student differences to enrich problem solving in my classroom? Opportunities for self-evaluation and revision
Survival Mode	**Eclectic Selection**
The "Life Raft" approach to teaching and materials: "If only we could find the perfect text or strategy" Focus and reliance on one thing, one right way, or one text	Eclectic strategies based on assessed needs of students Combinations of strategies and materials that meet the needs of a variety of learners Strategies that allow student choice and selection Integration of teaching and learning
Parts Thinking	**Holistic Thinking**
Fragmentation of time, effort, and skills Thinking about types of learners as one single thing Teaching skills in isolation Assuming student background will lead to a predictable outcome Teacher focus on error detection and the questioning of assumptions	Making connections on an regular basis for both concepts and life application Thinking about the current needs of learners Reassessing and choosing the "how to teach or demonstrate learning" strategies Connecting meaning through every lesson every day Checking student assumptions and student detection of error on a regular basis

BUILDING CONNECTIONS WITH STUDENTS

Two of the most important elements in successful literacy acquisition are relationship factors and teacher modeling (Tompkins, 2003). Literacy is learned, and learning takes place in an atmosphere of need where risk must be controlled for a student to benefit and accelerate learning. Ask yourself the following questions:

- Do your students have someone at school every day to speak and connect with on a personal level?
- Do you know who among your students had their basic survival needs met last night and who did not?

Relationships and Reinforcement

Kids know who cares and who does not. Students who seek out certain adults in our schools tell us a great deal about those adults, but what do students who do not seek anyone out tell us? Allowing hiding and invisibility is as bad as having no structure or routine. Some elementary teachers feel that every student in the classroom should be able to connect with them and know that the teacher is a caring person. Other adults operate differently, seeking out only those with whom they can easily form relationships. Elementary teachers working with students who do not connect with them will be serving those students well if they seek out mentors or significant others with whom the students can connect. Establishing a relationship with *any* positive adult is preferable to no relationships at all.

A Tale of Success: Winter 2003

An elementary staff in Colorado sat with the principal at a staff meeting early one morning. A teacher stood up and announced that it was that time of year for the "Two Minute Mentor" program (adapted from Assets Training & Character Education). Each staff member received a piece of paper and was asked to list one or two students who demonstrate certain listed characteristics. The characteristics include students who are very quiet in class or who do not have friends to play with outside of class.

Each staff member (not the child's teacher) chose a child with whom they could easily connect several times a week for about two minutes per meeting. Two teachers did a couple of role plays to help new staff know how the two-minute interaction ought to look and sound. Other staff members described past successes with this method. Students who still come back from middle school to visit a favorite mentor and report their current experiences are one example. Another example of success involved a parent who called to say that the elementary mentorship program helped their child through a rough transition to the middle or high school level. The program lasted from January through the next six weeks at the minimum. The staff has identified this as a very vulnerable period for quieter and more isolated students at their school. A staff member reported that the students benefit so much that the staff continues as long as the student wants and needs such contact.

Resiliency

Connections that impact a life do not have to take much time or cost much money. Connections that meet student needs and encourage positive behaviors can build resiliency and confidence in remarkable ways (see Table 2.2).

Table 2.2 Relationships that provide for student needs and positive behaviors

Type of Student Needs and Behaviors	What Works to Meet These Needs
1. Students feel a sense of control	• Give students meaningful choices • Let students negotiate conditions for learning or the relationship when appropriate
2. Students identify purpose	• Give students clarity in understanding purpose • Respect future purpose, but give current purpose as well • Explain hidden meanings or responses • Show relationships and connections
3. Students seek out support and reassurance	• Model respect • Cultural sensitivity and acceptance of differences • Use personal stories and events
4. Students take risks	• Keep the environment "humiliation free" • Keep private conversations private • Check on students frequently • Praise risk taking, however small • Respectful verbal and nonverbal communication
5. Students respond to reinforcement	• Specific praise • Celebrate success in a meaningful way • Celebrate the right things, higher stakes accomplishments
6. Students initiate contact	• Positive reinforcement • Unconditional regard • Model positive attributes you want the student to exhibit
7. Students choose to be cooperative	• Reinforce cooperative behaviors • Show connections of behavior to accomplishments • Show freedom and choices given when cooperation occurs
8. Students ask questions	• Praise questioning • Help students shape their questions for specificity and clarity • Ask students meaningful questions • Know when to answer and when to teach
9. Students seek freedom from chaos	• Provide organization • Rehearse order, use of tools, and finding needed materials • Provide methods of organization such as the use of color, space, and special materials
10. Students benefit from self-advocacy	• Teach the tools of negotiation • Students need to know their learning style and preferences • Students need to understand the impact of body language, words, and tone of voice

Resiliency is an essential characteristic of successful learners. Students who persevere even when things get tough are resilient. Students become resilient through positive relationships and reinforcement, especially with teachers. McCombs and Whistler (1997) cite "teachers' abilities to form more meaningful relationships with students—relationships that pay off in students' increased motivation, learning, and academic achievement." A classroom where teachers reinforce students for persevering is creative and supportive. In classrooms where organization and negotiation are modeled and taught, learning takes place more easily and with less interference. Also essential are equity and respect for diversity: "It is important that, as part of the negotiation, the culture of origin is not denigrated, but rather the ability to negotiate is seen as a survival tool for the work and school setting" (Payne, 2001, p. 107).

Students' attitudes about learning are highly influenced by caring adults, both in and outside of school. Students come to school with widely varied attitudes toward learning (McNeeley, Nonnemaker, & Blum, 2002). Not all home environments can stop survival-level activity long enough to provide a positive disposition to learning. Teachers, however, can influence what happens during the students' school hours and school days. Academic achievement and higher test scores do not originate with materials, teachers, or strategies. Student achievement starts with healthy connections to adults in positive learning environments where diversity is respected and is not just a buzzword or excuse.

THE BASIC TOOLKIT FOR TEACHERS OF DIVERSE LEARNERS

When we think about diverse groups of learners, it is difficult to establish hard and fast characteristics. We can use logic and experience to help us know when a student's verbal struggles result from disability; language acquisition; poverty; or other causes, and we can use specific strategies to accommodate that kind of learning struggle. Overall, however, it is easier to think in terms of both student struggles and student attributes or channels for learning. That way we can select strategies that allow students to experience learning success through their own individual attributes. We may argue that students need to learn from a variety of strategies, but it is essential that students learn success. Students who understand their own needs as learners benefit twice: once by getting adults to understand their needs and another time by providing self-adjusting techniques for themselves.

Basic Strategies for Accelerating Growth for All Learners

- Asking questions (teacher and students)
- Avoiding assumptions

- Asking for help from specialists provides variety
- Providing no-fault practice and rehearsal
- Designing for variety over short periods
- Making connections and establishing purpose
- Increasing vocabulary through concept-based learning
- Creating opportunities to integrate complex ideas
- Creating a respectful climate for learning
- Providing and requiring modeling and self-evaluation
- Using grouping size and composition to increase thinking levels
- Checking for, detecting, and correcting errors
- Organizing learning
- Accessing learning through multiple modalities, styles, or intelligences
- Using preassessment and formative assessment to make changes along the way
- Student goal setting, adjustment of goals, and evaluation of results

Basic Strategies for Accelerating Growth for Learners in Diverse Groups

We have organized our chart of research-based methods for diverse groups of learners by the roadblocks that should be avoided or removed as well as by the strategies that accelerate the growth of these particular students (see Table 2.3). The research sources for these strategies are also identified within the chart.

Table 2.3   Research-based strategies that accelerate learning for diverse groups of learners

Racial and Cultural Diversity Sources: Miller (2003); Stevenson, Howard, Coard, Wallace, and Brotman (2004); Stasz and Tankersley (2003); and Reissman (2001)	
Roadblocks to Literacy:	**Accelerating Student Growth:**
Prejudice and negative attitude	Establish an accepting climate
Preconceived attitudes, stereotypes	Use stories for many cultures and groups
Lack of respect	Use art and history to establish connections
Culturally specific experiences and language that are different from traditional U.S. language and experiences	Idiom avoidance
	Source of materials
	Ritual and celebration
	Peer coaching
Exposure to school-specific resources	Use of personal narratives
	Question assumptions as a rule
	Use situational or pun-based humor rather than personal and group humor

Table 2.3 (Continued)

Students Who Experience Poverty Sources: Payne (2001), Carter and Strickland (2001)	
Roadblocks to Literacy:	**Accelerating Student Growth:**
Don't know the hidden rules of the middle class Speak in causal registry as a rule Do not have emotional and spiritual resources May not have role models Basic survival needs may not be met Purpose for learning may not be established outside of school May have emotional reactions that do not include "school expected" control and attitude May not have access to health options May not be very mobile	Teach the differences between • Job language • Social language Rules personalized and relevant Build background knowledge Rules behind words Implications and unsaid assumptions Provide choice Project-based learning, integration of learning Small-group interaction Personnel connections and relationships Establish relevant purpose Acknowledge diversity and things teachers don't know Teach patterns and the exceptions to the patterns regarding both content and implications for content as well as for social situations Create translations between casual and formal registry (language) Clearly define when and where choice is possible Use personal goal setting and adjust goals as needed, then create opportunities for celebration
Special Education Students Sources: Kuzmich (1980, 1987), Andres and Lupart (1993), Council for Exceptional Children (2004), Pascopella (2003)	
Roadblocks to Literacy:	**Accelerating Student Growth:**
Has an identified disability that interferes with learning Needs accommodations and modifications that some teachers may not know how to deliver Stereotypes can interfere with learning Teacher expectations that are preset lower without benefit of fact Classrooms that support nondisabled students are not fluid or prone to change Parents level of expectations and knowledge of resources School's ability to provide adequate resources and accommodations	Cognitively Able with Learning Disabilities • Variable time • Variable response mode, such as verbal strategies versus mind mapping and other visual tools • Assisted structure and organization • Use of multiple intelligence strategies Cognitively Disabled • Content adjustment • Developmental stages • Multiple intelligences Physical Disabilities • Using cuing through sign, Braille, body language, etc. • Specialized assistance • Specialized access to materials and communication tools • Capitalizing on residual hearing, vision, and physical abilities where possible

Level of specialized service to provide replacement and compensatory skill development Student understanding of disability and learning needs	Emotional Disabilities • Cuing behavior • Specialized schedules • Specialized routines • Replacement strategies for anger or depression
Gifted and Talented Students **Sources: Sternberg (1996), Colorado Department** **of Education (2004), Torrance (1998)**	
Roadblocks to Literacy:	**Accelerating Student Growth:**
These may not match: • Student expectations and goals • Parent expectations and goals • Teacher expectations and goals Perseverance related to tasks that are not a passion or talent Perfectionism Student self-evaluation Student ability to self-advocate Pace Lack of choice	Teach: • Perseverance • Fluidity • Flexibility • Adaptability Teach students transforming or constructivist strategies Allow students to pursue passions and interests Foster creativity Self-created organizers Offer tiered assignments Establish learning contracts Don't hold back for the sake of the larger group or the "group experience" Preassess Compact or adjust time, content, and demonstrations of learning
Gender Differences **Sources: Smith and Wilhelm (2002), Brozo (2002), Blackburn (2003),** **Broughton and Fairbanks (2003)**	
Roadblocks to Literacy:	**Accelerating Student Growth:**
Boredom with selection of materials Seeing relevance and purpose Pace Resources and materials may not match interests and needs Lack of choice Lack of autonomy	Interest-based menus Integrated learning approaches Variable lengths of writing Varied types of writing Project- and problem-based learning Personal purpose and relevance Use of texts that are self-selected when possible, even within a prescribed genre or topic K–6: developing major language tasks (Epstein, 1978) 7–12: developing adaptive and reflective thinking (Paul & Elder, 2003)
English Language Learners **Sources: Gonzales (1995), Eakle (2003), Grognet (2000),** **McCune (2002), Benjamin (2002)**	
Roadblocks to Literacy:	**Accelerating Student Growth:**
The quirks of the English language, including inflection,	Use sheltered English strategies Visual representations

(Continued)

Table 2.3 (Continued)

idioms, possessives, gender, word order, unique sounds, and other confusing attributes Reinforcement of new language acquisition outside and inside school Speed of acquisition of survival level social language Skill of teachers and staff in dealing with English Language Learners Skill of teachers in introducing vocabulary and concepts to English-speaking students Teachers' understanding of root words, pronouns, expressions, metaphors, similes, and other hard-to-access ideas for English Language Learners Lack of privacy for a student to practice without embarrassment Norms to support nonbias behavior from students and staff Incorrect assumptions about groups of foreign students	Use of nonverbal cuing Schema Use effective research-based vocabulary strategies Teach • Phonological awareness • Phonemics • Fluency • Spelling Show and utilize language patterns Explain and demonstrate idioms, similes, and metaphors Demonstrate the implications of social language Use cross-linguistic strategies Allow penalty-free risk-taking and sheltered practice opportunities Give students some private or like group immersion time to practice Highlight word parts Early use of nouns and key verbs of action with gestures and pictures

YOU CAN'T LEARN TO READ WITHOUT READING

There are several important factors in setting up an educational environment that is conducive to literacy acquisition (Constantino, 1998). These include the following:

- Providing a wide variety of reading materials
- Providing adequate time for sustained reading with no other obligations, including writing or sharing
- Allowing student self-selection of reading materials by interest level
- Providing opportunities to pursue a favorite author, genre, or area of interest
- Allowing students to take books and materials home
- Providing appealing materials, books, colors, and pictures

Passports (see Table 2.4), tickets to reading, and literacy logs are all good ways to record and celebrate all the many books and materials

Table 2.4   A strategy for encouraging reading

Strategy: *Passports*

Literacy Competency: Functional Literacy, Content Literacy, and Critical Thinking Literacy.

Description: Use a passport to document the reading students do by genre or topic.

Advantages: Encourages reading and celebrates accomplishment of reading many books or other written materials over time. Increases fluency, language acquisition, vocabulary expansion, general knowledge, and specific content knowledge; also deepens understanding.

How to Use: Staple multiple half pages together with a cover, similar to the size of passport. Could also buy blank books in the "dollar"-type stores and cut them to size. Students put name and other information on one page; they could add a picture of themselves or draw one. Label each page with a favorite topic or genre. Students then record each title and author as they finish reading books and other materials. Pages can be stamped when full. Celebrations may include getting a book or magazine to take home and keep or earning time to read with a friend. The nature of the celebration should reflect the theme of reading as well.

Bottom-Line Examples:

⇑ This strategy works well for almost any type of learner.

⇒ This strategy would work for some special education students if some of the materials were also available on tape. Use tapes for early Braille readers, or hard-to-find materials in Braille for visually disabled students. English Language Learners who are at the survival level may also benefit from tapes and materials with plenty of picture clues.

⇓ This strategy does not work as well for cognitively or severely disabled students unless other media or assistance is offered. Cognitively disabled students should, however, be encouraged to read as much as possible, but they may need to start with functional or commercial signage, materials at an appropriate level, and other accommodations.

---

students read. The act of recording such items as title and author works well to allow a student a sense of pride in accomplishment. Color coding or assigning passport pages to genre or interest areas also helps students self-evaluate the type of reading toward which they gravitate.

Another factor in creating a climate for literacy is the arrangement of space. It is fun for elementary students to have a special spot in class to read other than their desk. It may be a corner of the room on the carpet near a friend. A cushion, a special chair, a square of carpet, a blanket, or a pile of stuffed animals can be used. Anything that attracts students is helpful, and it may vary with the age of the student.

Color and lighting are also important aspects of an environment that say, "Please read here." Changing the lighting to include lamps is more fun than just overhead fluorescent lighting, or perhaps you can create a scene that is seasonal, with a fake fireplace or a fantasy-type atmosphere or theme that relates to a class topic or genre.

When students have a choice of activities and ask to go to the reading area or center when they finish work, you have a true sign that the atmosphere is right and invites reading. Setting routines and expectations to manage behavior in the reading area will also be important. Habits of reading must be taught to many students who may not have had experiences outside of school settings. Students may need to rehearse the appropriate moves and skills with plenty of reinforcement for meeting the teacher's expectations.

YOU CAN'T LEARN TO WRITE WITHOUT WRITING

Well, we have discussed creating a climate for reading. What about writing? Writers crave cool things to write on or to write with. Special colored pencils or pens; writing implements of various size, texture, or thickness; journals; special pads of unique-sized paper, or paper with raised lines may tempt some students. Reluctant writers (and others) may prefer the computer as a writing tool or a smaller space in which to write, such as a sticky note or an advanced organizer. Desks work for some writers, but others prefer a clipboard on the floor, a laptop outdoors, a journal in a cozy corner, or a colorful theme-based center. Some students with disabilities may require special accommodations to make writing more accessible.

Doug Reeves (2000) notes that we must increase the amount of writing we ask students to do to improve writing. There are many ways we can increase the willingness of students to initiate writing tasks and seek out writing as a means of communication, celebration, and establishment of resources:

- Sending invitations to classmates and others, notes to relatives, and postcards home to describe accomplishments are all ways to use writing as a celebration rather than a drudgery.
- Color coding for multiple authors, feedback to peers with sticky notes, and highlighting favorite parts of a writing buddy's first draft are all great ways to use writing as a relationship building tool, not just a means to convey information or tell a story.
- Creating books and stories that can be illustrated by friends or younger students is fun. This can be done on the computer as well (see Table 2.5).

Table 2.5   A technology-based strategy for encouraging writing

---

Strategy: *Writers Club* (Webbe Books)

Literacy Competency: Functional Literacy, Technology Literacy.

Description: Creation of small storybooks or information books for younger readers using publishing programs to create small picture books or illustrated stories to share with younger classmates.

Advantages: Writing for others can be motivating, reinforces existing skills, helps form a sense of a community of learners, and introduces technology as having a purpose and benefit for others.

How to Use: Create an illustrated story or information book at the level your younger buddy can read. Work from a bank of words or a model book that your buddy could read easily. Use clear sequences and illustrations. Students can create pictures or use public domain illustrations from the Internet that help convey meaning. Younger students can rehearse reading this book with a partner or with their older buddy and then take it home as a gift.

Bottom-Line Examples:

⇑ This strategy works well for most elementary students in Grades 1–6.

⇒ This strategy would work for kindergartners as a verbal rehearsal if someone wrote for them or they attempted to write and others helped with corrections. This strategy does not work as well for visually impaired students but could be modified to include a story written on the computer with added sound effects. Many elementary students would need technology assistance.

⇓ Others students with certain types of impairments are not well-served by using this strategy. English Language Learners at the survival or non-English stage would not benefit from this strategy. However, books could be more of the dictionary type rather than the story type to assist with language acquisition.

Source: Used with permission from Thompson School District, Loveland, CO.

- Creating a class journal that everyone helps complete at the end of the day or week is a great activity and can even be shared with parents.
- Setting up e-mail pen pals and e-mailing parents and students also builds relationships and can instill a sense of writing as a key tool for communication.

We will cover types of writing and writing for a variety of audiences and purposes in upcoming chapters. However, using writing as a celebration and personal communication tool adds purpose, relevancy, and motivation for the beginning writer. Such positive attitudes also increase willingness of students to communicate through writing. A climate for writers is one that makes writing fun, important, and a natural part of communication.

YOU CAN'T LEARN TO SPEAK AND LISTEN WITHOUT SPEAKING AND LISTENING

Language practice through regular opportunities for speaking and listening directly impacts successful early reading. There are numerous studies that correlate the size of students' vocabulary and the indications of early reading success (Snow, Burns, & Griffin, 1998).

Early Literacy

We know that the comprehension of words emerges prior to the ability to produce those words in the first or second year of a child's life. Using Whitehead's (1967) developmental language stages, we can see the following progression of language acquisition and utilization:

Ages 2 to 4 years:	Transition from achievement of perception to acquisition of language
Ages 4 to 7 years:	Classification of thoughts, improved accuracy of perception
Ages 7 to 12 years:	Development of powers of observation tied to manipulation of the environment and thoughts
Ages 12 to 15 years:	Precision in language development, notions of scientific constants
Ages 15 to 17 years:	Generalization in language precision and in science, transfer to inferences and implications in real-life situations
Ages 17 years on:	Integration of past development with new knowledge, sophistication of the interrelationship of new and old experiences

So, what does this mean to educators? Most children with intact neurological systems who are exposed to language exhibit the skills necessary for reading success through speaking and listening first. The research on this is extensive and definitive. Educators have learned that speaking and listening must be an important part of a literacy program. We have journeyed through many eras of phonics versus whole language approaches and even types of spelling programs related to speech and phonemics. What we worry about currently is that the focus on getting students ready for high-stakes tests pulls us away from what we know about learning literacy. An all-or-nothing focus on the written word will not accelerate literacy in elementary-age children. Principals and instructional leaders need to reinforce our teachers who manage school days filled both with oral and written language opportunities and connections between oral and written language acquisition.

Metalinguistic Skills for Learners from Diverse Backgrounds

We need to give students opportunities throughout each day to practice metalinguistic skills: "These involve the ability not just to use language but to think about it, play with it, talk about it, analyze it componentially, and make judgments about acceptable versus incorrect forms" (Snow et al., 1998).

What does this look like in a classroom of students who come from different households and maybe even different countries? It is our belief that words and language are a part of an engaging, safe classroom climate. Students' ability to risk speech and interpretation is clearly related to an atmosphere of acceptance. Ruby Payne (2001) discusses classrooms where forms of speaking that are foreign to the teacher can be met with curiosity and discussed with respect. A classroom where students feel that the language spoken at home is somehow less than it should be will not be as open to learning as will those who are given situations and examples accepting of different forms of speaking. Payne discusses the difference between the language the child first learns and the language of the larger society. This may be so different as to cause difficulties in interpretation and the acquisition of meaning and situational use of language. She discusses the role of the teacher as one where the rules of language use are discussed through examples and stories.

The "Hidden" Rules of Language

Teachers who read stories to students do them a great service in listening and understanding language in many forms. However, many teachers ask questions about story content without using the opportunity to discuss the unique features of the language used in the story. This added line of questioning and discussion helps students learn about the "hidden" rules of language in a wonderful and nonthreatening context. Even though Pinnell and Fountas (1996) detail the use of "word walls" in their Guided Reading Book, they, like many others, caution against teaching words and language forms in isolation. We offer a strategy that makes play with language fun through the use of stories and word walls while employing a key strategy found to be very useful in guided or balanced reading programs (see Tables 2.6 and 2.7).

Table 2.6   A story- and play-based strategy for teaching the rules of English

---

Strategy: *English is a Funny Language*

Literacy Competency: Foundational Literacy, Critical Thinking Literacy, and Enterprising Literacy.

Description: Create a word "use" wall from a unique story or set of stories that illustrates the different rules of language use across cultures, languages, genre, or regions.

Advantages: Teaches students that language is fun to play with, that there are rules about when to use certain forms, and that diversity should be respected.

How to Use: Create a theme-based word use wall, choosing a particular genre of story such as fantasy of science fiction. Relate odd, unique, or fun words in the story to where it should be used and where it would be understood. See the example in Table 2.7 using Harry Potter and fantasy words. This strategy could work in any grade with modifications. The example in Table 2.7 is for upper elementary. For younger students, use pictures and icons to help with meaning and connections.

Sources and Further Research: (Pinnell & Fountas, 1996; Payne, 2001)

Bottom-Line Examples:

⇑ This strategy works well for students of poverty or non-English-speaking students as well as others who are developing a sense of language and its rules. This may include students who have not had rich family-based language experiences or who may have a linguistic disability.

⇒ This strategy would work for physically disabled students such as those who are deaf or blind, if accommodations and modifications are made to ensure their participation and access. Gifted linguistic learners will see connections rapidly and may need alternative prompts or activities to do along with the theme-based word wall.

⇓ This strategy does not work as well for severely cognitively disabled students.

Table 2.7   The funny thing about English words

Source	Word	Means	Other Words (Synonyms)	When to Use
Harry Potter books	Muggle	Someone who does not have magic powers	Mortal	In stories about things that are not real
Students in our school	Bad	Someone we think does things that we admire	Cool Rad or Radical Good Wicked	Use with friends in conversation or in dialogue portion of a story
Television programs	I reckon	Someone who understands or gets the unstated idea	I could I get it I understand I would think that . . .	Use in creating a dialogue for a script or story; you could also use this in conversation with a friend, but not in a job interview
Students in our school	Sweet!	Really good	Good Great Awesome	Use with friends in conversation or in dialogue portion of a story
Students in our school	Kickin'	Great, as in "We had a kickin' time at the party."	Fun Enjoyable Amusing Entertaining	Use with friends in conversation or in dialogue portion of a story

READING, WRITING, SPEAKING, AND LISTENING EVERY DAY

In this time of extremely diverse classrooms, a language experience and group writing experience may be more complicated as we try to help students construct meaning and relationships. This will take techniques that we know to a different level. We may need to modify known strategies to take greater diversity into account. Two-column note taking is a wonderful introduction to note taking in Grades 2 and 3, but we may need to add examples and pictures rather than definitions only to help more learners access content-specific vocabulary.

Creating opportunities to play with words and dialogue prior to using such a strategy will further enhance it. The brain craves rehearsal prior to action. Verbal modeling and practice help students reach higher levels of thinking (Paul & Elder, 2001). Turning to a partner to rehearse what you will write or role-playing a dialogue prior to reading or writing will cause better written results.

Speaking and listening are also essential follow-up tools. Remember when some of our moms told us to read stories or assignments out loud so we could hear whether we had the right words? Well, they were prompting us to use a highly effective strategy. More specifically, they were prompting us to use a strategy that is highly effective for some learners, whereas others may be better served by listening to someone else read their work or by color highlighting. The key is to connect speaking and listening to everyday literacy in a variety of ways to create a classroom climate that enhances and accelerates literacy learning for all students.

Knowing the 3
Literacy Learner

When we look at individual learners, we know that each one is unique with special qualities in varying degrees. Because each has grown in his or her own environment and has been socialized in a particular way, each learner has preferences and comfort zones in the learning process. There are other circumstances that add diversity to a learner's individual profile as well, including culture, poverty, first language, and special needs.

BRAIN RESEARCH

The brain has become a focus for educators through which we can view our practice and make instructional, assessment, and curricular decisions. Although every brain is unique, there are some commonalities about the brain that connect to literacy and help us remain mindful of how the brain's operations support the development of literacy skills. Educators can use this information to their advantage in planning and designing learning that will help students be successful.

Man has an instinctive ability toward oral communication, as we see even in the sounds of very young babies, but there is no real inclination to write or read. At an early age, we seem to be "wired for sound" but not naturally for print. In young children, communication is a survival skill, and children are genetically predisposed to learn a language. The brain has earmarked a large number of neurons specifically for this purpose.

When we think about the formal teaching of reading and writing, we must consider how the human mind works. If every child could learn to read without effort, we would not have to think about brain research as a guide for teaching reading, writing, speaking, and listening. But every child and brain is unique. Synthesizing the work of such notable educators and researchers as Pat Wolfe, David Sousa, Barbara Given, Robert Sylwester, and Geoffery and Renata Caine, we can suggest nine core factors linked to how the brain learns and then discuss their implications for literacy to help teachers make better choices for designing learning in the classroom:

1. Pattern recognition and schema

2. Emotions

3. Parallel processing

4. Entire physiology

5. The search for meaning

6. Wholes and parts

7. Social learning

8. Conscious and unconscious attention

9. Every brain is unique

Pattern Recognition and Schema

The brain operates on probability based on past experiences. It has the ability to recognize and construct patterns to identify the familiar or not so familiar by relying on schemas that have been formed from prior knowledge and experiences.

Schemas are patterns, clusters, arrangements, and categories that are stored together and understood. This is how we develop concepts by identifying like attributes or ideas. For example, Thanksgiving may be a concept that students have. Yet Thanksgiving is also a holiday, and the concept of holiday includes Christmas, Hanukkah, and Fourth of July. Chaining is taking concepts that have a commonality and linking them together. Mel Levine (1990) refers to this as "horizontal threading." The brain naturally looks through its filing system to access other ideas and concepts that may be related to the new learning. The brain usually will reject meaningless patterns, such as bits of information that are unrelated to what it already knows or finds interesting.

Implications for Literacy

Past experiences are unique and specific to each learner. Children from other cultures and religious backgrounds may not understand the following if they read it in a story:

Pat took his Hanukkah money and walked down the street to the mall. On his way he passed the french fry van and had to stop and get a hot treat smothered with vinegar.

This is not a passage that elicits comprehension without the schemas one needs to decipher it. Meaning comes from making connections, and, without schemas, students' connections are not complete.

Schemas are also useful in spelling as they are linked to rules and usual patterns that have been established. Helping students develop schemas has long been used to help English language learners with the quirky challenges of English where so many rules and schemas are skewed by exceptions. Schemas can be helpful in making predictions, patterns, and connections when students are learning something new. Strategies for teachers to influence pattern-making include the following:

- Presenting schemas for writing
- Embedding grammar and spelling in context
- Integrating literacy skills through the curriculum
- Ensuring that literacy skills have real-world applications

The other literacy aspect that schemas support is the integration of language skills embedded in contextual material. Whole language was a valid concept that was not implemented with great understanding by teachers. It did not mean that we were laissez-faire when it came to phonics, spelling, and grammatical skills, but we should have been teaching them as part of the reading and writing process and not as discrete entities or ignoring them as if they didn't matter.

Emotions Are Critical to the Learning Process

We cannot separate emotions from the learning process (Ornstein & Sobel, 1987). What and whether we learn is dependent on our state of mind, emotions, expectations, and personal sense of efficacy. Emotions help with the storage of memories and the recall process. Emotional impacts have a really powerful effect upon whether something has the ability to be recalled.

Implications for Literacy

The emotional climate that is set for the literacy classroom is crucial to student success. It is essential for teachers and students to be supportive and cooperative in the classroom. High levels of frustration or anxiety will not aid in the learning process and may actually turn individual students against reading and writing in the future. Encouragement and a nonthreatening climate are essential to help learners persist in language acquisition.

Parallel Processing

The brain takes in huge "gulps" of stimuli simultaneously (Ornstein & Thompson, 1984), referred to as "parallel processing": "The ability of the brain to process information down multiple paths, using multiple modes simultaneously, is what gives us our enormous capacity for detecting patterns and forming mental maps" (Parry & Gregory, 2003). Parallel processing may appear to be somewhat messy and random, but that is how the brain works. It is much more like a complex, jungle ecosystem than a linear computer process.

Implications for Literacy

When reading, the brain is using schemas that have formed in the past. The brain is thereby relying on phonological awareness and phonemics, sight words, contextual and pictorial clues, as well as predictable repetition in text (see Figure 1.1 in Chapter 1). For example, when reading a story, students may switch from one way of interpreting words to another as required to make sense of the text. They may use their phonics skills to attack an unknown word as well as recognize some words from sight. By looking at an illustration of a truck, they may acknowledge that the truck is a garbage truck and that it knocked over the "garbage" rather than the "garage." They may also know that the last sentence on the page probably reads, "So what else could happen?" because the previous pages ended that way and a pattern has been formed. When teachers understand the concept of parallel processing, they are able to orchestrate multiple opportunities for making meaning.

Learning Involves the Entire Physiology

Learning can be as natural as breathing. The brain seeks new information and remains curious and self-motivating if opportunity, relevance, personal meaning, or novelty are present. Neuron growth, nourishment, and synaptic connections are intrinsically connected to the perception and interpretation of experiences (Diamond & Hopson, 1998). Threat and stress negatively influence the brain, whereas high-challenge, happiness, and contentment have positive effects and facilitate learning (Ornstein & Sobel, 1987). The brain is very susceptible to school, home, and life experiences that are either positive or negative. Any experiences that affect our emotions affect our learning.

Implications for Literacy

Each brain is unique based on life experiences and emotional situations. Not all students are at the same level of maturation at the same chronological age. There may be up to five years' difference in maturation between any two "average students." Attributing "delays" in reading to chronological age without considering developmental growth may not be accurate and may cause undo anxiety and stress both in students and parents.

Searching for Meaning

The search for meaning is a basic survival instinct. The brain recognizes the familiar and also looks for novelty (O'Keefe & Nadel, 1978). This occurs while we are awake or asleep. It is impossible to shut this search down. The best we can do is to channel this quest and help the learner focus.

Implications for Literacy

This challenges teachers' ability to structure an environment that is familiar yet has novelty, challenge, and investigative capacity. Literacy programs must build on the familiar while creating a sense of wonderment and challenge. Engagement in reading, writing, and speaking about, as well as listening to interesting and relevant topics, is crucial to intrigue the learner (see also Chapter 7 on Innovative Literacy).

The Brain Pays Attention to Wholes and Parts

All students have two hemispheres in their brains: one left hemisphere and one right hemisphere, which are different but continually interactive no matter what is being processed (Springer & Deutsch, 1985; Hart, 1975). Thus teachers need to realize that whereas the left hemisphere tends to reduce information into parts, the right prefers the whole.

Implications for Literacy

Although phonics, vocabulary, spelling, and grammar need to be learned to facilitate growth in the reading and writing process, they are better taught in context and incorporated into real-life, whole language experiences. The pieces don't make nearly as much sense to the brain if they are not embedded in real language.

Social Learning

The need to connect, associate, collaborate, and cooperate is prevalent in all humans as well as in other species (Panksepp, 1998). We tend to place value on independence and interdependence as positive human traits (Covey, 1989). There are basically two social subsystems; one focused on the dyadic relationships (this begins at birth) and the second focused on group relationships, which come later (Harris, 1998).

Implications for Literacy

Because social interactions rely so heavily on communication, it is only natural that classrooms should facilitate both social interaction and opportunities for oral and written communication. Buddy reading, peer editing, and round-robin reading are all ways to facilitate both social and literacy skills development at the same time.

Learning Involves Conscious and Unconscious Attention

The brain is constantly scanning the environment to make sense out of the world (Sylwester, 1995; Deporter, Reardon, & Singer-Nourie, 1998). Peripheral stimuli include everything from body language to classroom climate to physical environment, including décor and orderliness. This occurs at a subconscious level but still registers with the brain. It is not only the intended that conveys a message; it is everything that happens overtly or covertly, spoken or unspoken.

Implications for Literacy

All the subtleties in the classroom, from the bulletin boards and displays of student work to the tone of voice of the teacher, affect student response to learning. Orderly classrooms that help with the use of support structures, such as charts, diagrams, word walls, and visuals, help students in the acquisition of literacy skills. The teacher's enthusiasm for and modeling of reading, writing, speaking, and listening influence students on an unconscious level, communicating both the joy and value of acquiring literacy skills. What we do often screams louder than what we say.

Every Brain Is Unique

Although every brain operates in basically the same way, each one is unique. This is a result of nature and nurture. Our genetic makeup and different experiences and environments have influenced and constructed our brains differently over time. These differences play out through learning styles and different strengths in areas of intelligence.

Implications for Literacy

This should be a caution to educators not to simply accept one program or one method for developing literacy skills. It encourages us to treat the learner as an individual. We want to know that learner, identify their areas of strength, identify their learning needs and preferences, and then capitalize on that knowledge to create learning that will intrigue, engage, and facilitate growth.

DEVELOPMENTAL STAGES

We know that children mature individually and that there may be up to five years' variance in children when we examine growth. If we synthesize what we know about children's generalized developmental stages of growth (Wood, 1994) and apply that to what we know about their growth as readers, writers, and literacy learners, then we can use that information to observe our students and to differentiate targets and expectations for them (see Table 3.1).

The overall synthesis shown in Table 3.1 is only a guideline. Students can and will vary in their individual stages of development. As we further observe student characteristics, capabilities, and needs as readers and writers, we will be able to recognize their individual status and progress from emerging to developing to fluent (see Tables 3.2 and 3.3).

Table 3.1   Developmental readiness for reading and writing for ages 5–12

The Learner	Reading	Writing
Five-year-olds • One thing at a time • Helpful • Empathetic • Literal • Learn through play	Big books Short chapter read-alouds Predictable books Peer reading Phonics instruction Read the "room"	Draw and label Initial consonants spelling Difficulty with pencil (fine motor not well developed) Love to write about their world
Six-year-olds • Active • Competitive • Industrious • Eager to learn	Predictable and easy chapter books Peer reading important Phonics and whole language	Drawing and writing Letter spelling "I lke sup" Writing in a "hurry" Like fantasy, pets, and friends
Seven-year-olds • Focused • Often insecure • Cautious • Language growth • Precision	Subvocalized More individual reading Phonics increase Reading comprehension focus	Longer stories, beginning, middle, and end Correct spelling begins Nonfiction writing Content areas

(Continued)

Table 3.1 (Continued)

The Learner	Reading	Writing
Eight-year-olds • High energy • Gregarious • Resilient • Talkative • Industrious	Heterogeneous groups based on interests Independent reading Longer chapter books	New genres (poetry, cartoons, etc.) Drafts and revisions emerge Spelling improves (sources) Chapter books Cursive writing
Nine-year-olds • Competitive • Worrier • Concerned with fairness • Descriptive • Self-critical, need encouragement and laughter	Reading groups continue Beginnings of research Dictionary skills taught Enjoyment of poetry	Introduce writing process Use of dictionary Broader themes Increasing fluent handwriting
Ten-year-olds • Growth spurt • Emotional extremes • Strong sense of right and wrong • Good listeners • Ability to abstract	Enjoys poetry and trade books Independent reading a favorite activity High interest in comics	Longer poems Longer chapter books Note taking Fluent cursive writing
Eleven-year-olds • Need more sleep • Need to save face • Fine motor ability • Emotional extremes • Like to work with others • Emerging adult role awareness • Test limits	Trade books with longer assignments Likes biographies Likes to read to others Responds positively to fiction and nonfiction	Opportunity to rehearse writing in various forms: poetry, cartoons, reports, etc. Spelling more accurate Functional handwriting
Twelve-year-olds • High energy • Enthusiastic • Self-aware, somewhat secure • Peers important • Enjoys conversation • Particular abilities emerge • High interest in current events and the world	Trade books, newspapers, and magazines Reading for information Synthesizing from several sources Library skills apparent	Functional spelling Teen issues begin to dominate Summarization and clarity appears in writing Word processing used in writing

For more information, see Wood (1994).

Table 3.2   Status of readers at different fluency levels

Emerging Reader	Developing Reader	Fluent Reader
Left to right eye movement Top to bottom eye movement Knows consonants: both initial and final Uses pictures for clues Knows letters and words Has a sight word vocabulary Knows some punctuation Somewhat insecure Lacks confidence Lacks comprehension skills Has difficulty decoding words	Is a confident reader Decodes with skill Uses background information linked to new information Reads at grade level Self-corrects Thinks about what he or she is reading Knows what he or she has read and can discuss details	Loves to read Reads avidly Exhibits good vocabulary Decodes easily and automatically Self-corrects Engages in higher-order thinking Interprets meaning and purposes of reading Likes various genres
Needs Lots of opportunities for partner reading and modeling Celebration of growth Continual phonics instruction Experience chart writing and reading	**Needs** Continued growth through more challenging materials Choice to increase engagement Continue development of word-attack skills Provide variety of genres	**Needs** Offer increasingly more challenging reading materials and genres High-interest books Buddy reading to share expertise with others Book clubs

Table 3.3   Status of writers at different fluency levels

Emerging Writer	Developing Writer	Fluent Writer
Writes stories from pictures Moves from scribbling to symbols to letters Moves left to right Talks his or her writing Begins to invent spelling Chooses topics he or she likes to write about	Moves from invented to regular spelling More accurate with use of letters, beginning and ending Uses models of writing that are familiar Recognizes beginnings, middles, and endings	Loves to write Writes in many forms Uses story structures Recognizes conventions and uses them appropriately Subject and verb agreement Edits and revises Seeks resources for information
Needs Opportunities to write regularly Partner and small group writing Phonics instruction Self-selection of topics Intriguing writing materials to engage the writer	**Needs** To hear a variety of writing genres Daily writing Modeling of the writing process Self-selection of topics Peer and small group editing	**Needs** Teacher models of all types of genres Self-selection of topics To engage daily in the whole process of writing Instruction on revisions

LEARNING STYLES

Teachers have known about diverse learning styles for many years. Although there is no scientific evidence of student achievement related to the attention paid to learning styles, millions of teachers will attest to increased student engagement and motivation when the classroom honors diverse learners. Students who feel comfortable, included, and respected are more likely to learn and flourish.

The Clipboard, the Puppy, the Microscope, and the Beach Ball

In this series of books (Gregory & Chapman, 2002; Gregory, 2003; Gregory & Kuzmich, 2004), we have used four analogies to represent four different learning styles: the clipboard, the puppy, the microscope, and the beach ball.

These four categories incorporate key aspects of several learning style frameworks (Gregorc, 1982; Kolb, 1984; Strong, Silver, Perini, & Tuculescu, 2002; McCarthy, 1990, 2000). Table 3.4 illustrates the connections and similarities of the theoretical frameworks. We think the clipboard, puppy, microscope, and beach ball are probably easier to remember and do a good job of representing each style's attributes. For more detail about each style's general learning preferences and learning needs, see Table 3.5. For how those preferences affect their learning in reading, writing, speaking, and listening, see Table 3.6.

Gender Issues

Gender also plays a role in how and what students learn. Sadker (2002) notes that two-thirds of all students placed in special education classes are males, and Smith and Wilhelm (2002) identified trends showing the following:

- Some boys take longer to read than girls
- Girls read more than boys
- Girls value reading more than boys
- Boys often consider themselves nonreaders

Gender interaction with learning styles is also relevant to consider here. Newkirk (2002) notes that males who have learning problems and are low-achieving are often identified as "visual learners and require multimodal approaches to literacy learning—yet relatively few teachers are comfortable enough with visual storytelling to make this an option" (Newkirk, 2002, p. 174).

Table 3.4   A matrix of learning styles illustrates their connections and similarities

	Gregorc, 1982	Kolb, 1984	Silver et al., 2000	4Mat/ McCarthy, 2000
Beach Ball	Concrete Random • Divergent • Experiential • Inventive	Accommodator • Likes to try new ideas • Values creativity, flexibility, and risk takers	Self-Expressive • Feelings to construct new ideas • Produces original and unique materials	Type 4 Dynamic • Create and act • Usefulness and application of learning
Clipboard	Concrete Sequential • Task oriented • Efficient • Detailed	Converger • Values what is useful and relevant, immediacy, and organizing essential information	Mastery • Absorbs information concretely, and processes step by step	Type 3 Common Sense • Think and do • Active, practical • Make things work
Microscope	Abstract Sequential • Intellectual • Analytical • Theoretical	Assimilator • Avid readers who seek to learn • Patience for research • Values concepts	Understanding • Prefers to explore ideas and use reason and logic based on evidence	Type 2 Analytical • Reflect and think • Observers who appreciate lecture methods
Puppy	Abstract Random • Imaginative • Emotional • Holistic	Diverger • Values positive, caring environments that are attractive, comfortable, and people-oriented	Interpersonal • Appreciates concrete ideas and social interaction to process and use knowledge	Type 1 Imaginative • Feel and reflect • Create and reflect on an experience

Source: Adapted with permission from *Data Driven Differentiation in the Standards-Based Classroom* by Gayle H. Gregory and Lin Kuzmich. Thousand Oaks, CA: Corwin Press, © 2004. www.corwinpress.com

Table 3.5   Learning styles and their preferences and needs

Styles	Learning Preferences	Needs
Beach Ball **Abstract Random** Self-expressive 	Like choice Like spontaneity Like freedom Like variety Like multiple resources Like open-ended assignments Like adaptive environments Imaginative and creative opportunities	Structure and routine to complete assignments Timelines and rubrics Agendas and contracts to stay on task Clear expectations to keep learner on track
Puppy **Concrete Random** Interpersonal 	Like supportive environment Like encouraging teachers Like shared decision making Like working with colleagues Like peer tutoring Like empathic listeners Like safe classrooms	Need to develop independent reading Reading to help them understand themselves and others
Clipboard **Concrete Sequential** Logical 	Like teacher direction Like practical information Like organization and structure Like consistent routines and procedures Like concrete examples Like real experiences Like precision and accuracy	Need to develop tolerance for ambiguity Branch out from practical to more fantasy-based reading materials
Microscope **Abstract Sequential** Analytical 	Like concepts, models, and symbols Like serious, logical, structured work Like big picture and details Like lectures and reading for information Like investigation and research Like analytical assignments Like independent work	Prefer charts, graphs, and organizers Need interesting material with detail Need advance organizers to see the big picture

Table 3.6   Four learning styles and their preferences for reading, writing, speaking, and listening

Styles	Reading Preferences	Writing Preferences	Speaking and Listening
Beach Ball **Abstract Random** Self-expressive	Likes variety of reading materials Needs a "hook" to focus Sees the big picture Imagination and fiction Science fiction Adventure Interesting reading Poetic and creative	Metaphors Imagination and fiction, including science fiction and fantasy Self-expression and personal opportunities to use imagination and symbolism Variety and choice are important	Spontaneous conversation about things that intrigue Opportunities to listen to interesting ideas from others Brainstorming Using creative and metaphorical language
Puppy **Concrete Random** Interpersonal	Likes stories that have personal feelings and interesting people Biographies Likes to relate their reading to their own lives Enjoys discussions and interpretations of reading Likes peer- and buddy-guided reading	Enjoy interviews Letter writing Collaborative writing Personal feedback Enjoys sharing personal feelings and those of others	Conversations about feelings and emotions Discussions about people Listening to others' ideas, thoughts, and feelings Think, Pair, Share
Clipboard **Concrete Sequential** Logical	Personal engagement Likes to read for practical reasons and information. (e.g., How to . . .) Prefers reality Likes guided reading with teacher direction Responds to reading to find out information	Likes to write to report or organize information Likes to write for practical purposes Real-life situations Appreciates guidelines, models, examples, and organizers	Likes to ask and answer questions about specific information and ideas Likes to listen to details
Microscope **Abstract Sequential** Analytical	Independent reading on topic of interest Likes details and description Likes challenges and intrigue in books Likes graphs, charts, and lists Likes to process and question reading Reads for information	Essays Analytical pieces that require logic and are supported with research and evidence Likes to provide detail and description in writing Likes to create rationales and use or find support evidence	Needs encouragement to engage in dialogue Appreciates deeper discussions that analyze ideas and clarify thinking

Drawing, storyboarding, graphic organizers, and cartooning work well for these learners. Mind mapping is a great tool to identify features of a concept, process, or idea or to illustrate the plot or theme of a reading.

GARDNER'S MULTIPLE INTELLIGENCES

Howard Gardner's theory of Multiple Intelligence (MI) is another lens through which we know our students. Gardner's MI formulation is evolving over time, but we are working here with eight ways of being smart (Gardner, 1983):

The first two intelligences are *communication* oriented:

1. Verbal/Linguistic: an affinity for literacy and the natural ability to read, write, speak, and listen

2. Musical/Rhythmic: using rhythm, rhyme, beat, rap, dance, and song as a means of making meaning in learning and life and as a communication tool

The next four are *object* related:

3. Logical/Mathematical: a way of thinking and processing that includes the use of logic, reason, organization, and patterning

4. Visual/Spatial: using visual representation to process information through pictures, mind maps, and visualization

5. Bodily/Kinesthetic: internalizing information and concepts through body or muscle movement and hands-on involvement

6. Naturalist: recognizing patterns in nature and the ability to recognize like attributes and classify or categorize

The last two deal with *the self*:

7. Interpersonal: the ability to work with others, share, and cooperate using natural social skills

8. Intrapersonal: the ability to work independently and monitor self through reflection and metacognition

Figure 3.1   Each of the multiple intelligences can be identified and associated with a
particular area of the brain

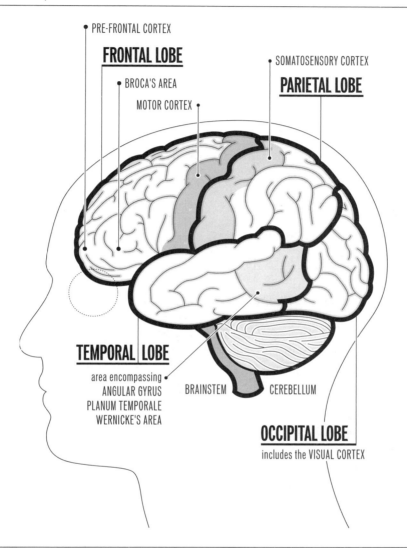

Multiple Intelligences and the Brain

Brain research also changes rapidly, but we can associate each of the
eight intelligences with particular areas of the brain (see Figure 3.1):

1. Verbal/Linguistic: left temporal and frontal lobes

2. Musical/Rhythmic: right temporal lobe

3. Visual/Spatial: occipital and parietal regions (right hemisphere more dominant)

4. Logical/Mathematical: left frontal and right parietal lobes

5. Bodily/Kinesthetic: cerebellum, basal ganglia, motor cortex

6. Naturalist: left parietal lobe (this area helps identify living and nonliving things)

7. Interpersonal: frontal lobes, temporal lobe (in right hemisphere), limbic system

8. Intrapersonal: frontal lobes, parietal lobes, limbic system

Thomas Armstrong suggests that literacy involves the whole brain: "Certain distinctive brain structures, particularly in the left hemisphere for most people, are particularly important when it comes to the processing of the phonological, semantic, and syntactic aspects of words. In sum, there are strong reasons for literacy to be regarded as part and parcel of linguistic intelligence" (Armstrong, 2003).

The areas of the brain associated with speech include Broca's area, Wernicke's area, the angular gyrus, the primary visual area, and the motor cortex. Visual (written) information enters through the optic nerve, and the thalamus directs it to the occipital area where spatial intelligence is interpreted. Then it relays to the angular gyrus, where the temporal, parietal, and occipital lobes intersect. It is suggested that people who have trouble with reading and writing have confusion at this location in the brain (Horwitz, Rumsey, & Donahue, 1998). Wernicke's area is where all this incoming information is synthesized, interpreted, and understood. It then proceeds to Broca's area, where it is embedded in the grammatical system. There it uses a program to facilitate articulation, and then the motor cortex triggers the muscles in the lips, tongue, and larynx so that actual words can be spoken (Geschwind, 1979).

Although this activity takes place in the brain's left hemisphere, there is evidence that the right hemisphere is also involved. The emotional right hemisphere is known to be stimulated when the following occur:

- Reading material evokes emotions, feelings, anxiety, or passion (Van Strien, Stolk, & Zuiker, 1995)
- The reader is selecting appropriate words (Coney & Evans, 2000)
- The reader uses information from the left hemisphere to interpret and understand the material (Coney, 1998)

Multiple Intelligences Working Together

Clearly, the multiple intelligences are working together to create language. During reading, learners are using the following:

1. Verbal/Linguistic: intelligence to make the appropriate letter-sound relationships

2. Musical/Rhythmic: as the sounds and rhymes play with the reader

3. Visual/Spatial: as they picture and image in the mind what is described in the text

4. Logical/Mathematical: for organization and syntax, and for thinking critically about the information

5. Bodily/Kinesthetic: as the reader internalizes the content

6. Naturalist: as nature sounds and images emerge

7. Interpersonal: for interpretation of feelings, emotions, and actions evoked by the reading

8. Intrapersonal: as readers reflect and connect with their past experience and their own lives

Different Ways of Being Smart

As students vary in their unique combinations and strengths of the multiple intelligences, they may have more affinity or less comfort with aspects of reading and writing. Some may have less strength in the verbal-linguistic area, causing them to struggle with letter and word relationships, but may have real strength in visual/spatial intelligence.

As teachers, how do we use knowledge of those strengths and put them to best use to increase the reading and writing abilities of the learner? In Table 3.7, we suggest how the characteristics and tendencies of students with "different ways of being smart" relate to literacy learning.

Table 3.7   Multiple intelligences and literacy

Verbal/Linguistic

Reads fluently, voraciously, and easily
Writes easily and well
Enjoys reading
Speaks easily and is articulate
Appreciates communication
Shares opinion with evidence
Listens attentively
Loves lovely language

Musical/Rhythmic

Enjoys rhyme and rhythm in words
Uses rhythm to spell and remember
    vocabulary and write
Chunks through rhythm
Likes to use songs, raps, and rhyme to embed
    and remember new information
Appreciates background music as they work,
    read, or write
Appreciates nature sounds and the impact of
    music related to stories or reading material

Visual/Spatial

Loves to illustrate
Likes to use highlight while reading
Color coding
Creates visual pictures as they read
Sees the character and all details
    in their mind
Enjoys mind mapping
Sees in vivid color
Likes visual technology
Interprets in picture
Uses visual descriptive language
    in writing and speaking

Logical/Mathematical

Likes to organize before writing
Appreciates structure and routines in writing
Likes clear, precise language and expectations
Uses logic and critical thinking
Likes to solve problems
Enjoys plots, challenges, and intrigue in stories
Likes to problem solve

Bodily/Kinesthetic

Prefers movement and involvement to
    deepen understanding
Prefers hands-on interpretation
Likes to manipulate
Likes to demonstrate and create
Appreciates role-playing

Naturalist

Appreciates nature and books with
    descriptive nature
Tends to organize and make connections
    through categorizing
Notices patterns in nature and elsewhere
Sees detail in setting and plot

Interpersonal	Intrapersonal
Enjoys conversations and peer reading and editing Makes connections with characters Makes meaning through dialogue and debating and discussing ideas Is social and enjoys biographies and cultural aspects Empathizes with others	Prefers to work independently Becomes reflective and self-absorbed Enjoys journal writing and reflective activities Sets goals and plans for personal growth Requires opportunity to make meaning personally through personal involvement

BEST TEACHING PRACTICES FOR ALL LEARNING STYLES, PREFERENCES, AND INTELLIGENCES

Rather than trying to identify and cater to each of the learning styles and multiple intelligences, teachers need to help *all* students feel comfortable and capable in the literacy classroom.

Give Students the Why, What, How, and So What

We can offer the following four suggestions:

1. *Give students the Why:* Substantiate or rationalize learning as a desirable skill or necessary knowledge. Give them a reason for reading and writing. Connect to their world, and make the literacy experiences relevant, useful, and meaningful.

2. *Give students the What:* Give them the facts. Provide models and concepts. Provide time to explore. Make sure substance and content are clearly exposed, shared, and examined. Model reading and writing for students, and give them examples, organizers, and samples. Help all learners see the big picture, and scaffold the learning to better ensure success.

3. *Give students the How:* Provide time for practice and practical application of the skills of reading and writing. Provide ample experimentation and application in practical ways to use new knowledge and skills in their lives.

4. *Give students the So What:* Offer outlets for creativity and dynamic interaction with the material and skills.

Allow Students to Make Choices

Allowing students to select opportunities brings the learning styles into active use (see also the following choice boards). Whether for reading or for writing, students like to express themselves and to make their own choices based on personal preferences (see Tables 3.8 and 3.9).

Use High-Payoff Instructional Strategies

Robert Marzano's research (Marzano et al., 2001) across all subject disciplines and age groups shows that the following nine strategies have a large impact on student achievement:

1. Using similarities and differences, analogies, and metaphors

2. Summarizing and note taking

3. Reinforcing effort and providing recognition

4. Assigning homework and practice

5. Generating nonlinguistic representations

6. Using cooperative learning

7. Setting objectives and providing feedback

8. Generating and testing hypotheses

9. Providing questions, cues, and advanced organizers

We discussed these strategies and their link to literacy tactics in greater detail in Chapter 1 (see Table 1.4), but it bears repeating here that these strategies should probably get on every teacher's "best dressed" list. We incorporate these strategies and the literacy tactics linked to them throughout this book as high-payoff ways to support accelerated growth and achievement for all learners.

Table 3.8   Writing survey

1. I often feel like _____ when I'm asked to write.

2. I would say I'm a _____ kind of writer.

3. I think _____ is a good writer because _____.

4. I like writing when _____.

5. It would be fun to write if _____.

6. It's easy for me when _____.

7. I find it hard to _____.

8. My favorite writing spot is _____.

9. It would help me if _____.

10. I would like to write about these things _____.

What else would you like to know from your students?

_____

_____

_____

_____

_____

_____

_____

_____

_____

Table 3.9   Reading inventory suggestions

1. I like to read because _____.

2. I spend my free time _____.

3. I don't like to _____.

4. My favorite books are _____.

5. At home I read _____.

6. It's hard for me at school to _____.

7. The easiest thing about school is _____.

8. I am reading _____.

9. _____.

10. _____.

Choice Boards

Teachers may use choice boards to enable students to tap into areas of strength and comfort and also to prescribe opportunities to stretch in areas that need attention. Choice boards may be used with the multiple intelligences (see Table 3.10), or for assignments linked to stories (see Table 3.11), book reviews (see Table 3.12), or other activities.

Verbal/linguistic intelligence will be part of any choice students make, but in the case of a story assignment, for example (see Table 3.11), it can take many different forms, including the following:

- A poster that describes the characters and plot
- A skit or dialogue that shares the content
- A diorama representing a key event or turning point in the story
- A graphic organizer or time line showing the events (Kidspiration or Inspiration Software may be used)
- A ballad that tells the story
- An interview with a key character
- A talk show where key characters partake in a dialogue
- An audiotape or videotape
- A comparison with a recently read story showing similarities and differences

As long as the teacher provides clear outcomes or expectations when planning any instructional or rehearsal practice, choice boards can allow differentiated learning linked to all learning styles and multiple intelligences.

GENDER ISSUES

Although we have been examining learners in general, we also realize that gender plays a role in how and what students learn.

We Know from the work of Smith and Wilhelm (2002) that research shows that there are trends to indicate that:

- some boys take longer to read than girls
- girls read more than boys
- girls value reading more than boys
- boys often consider themselves nonreaders.

Sadker (2002) notes that two thirds of all students placed in special education classes are male. Learning styles are relevant to consider here. Newkirk (2002) notes that males who have learning problems and are low-achieving are often identified as "visual learners and require multimodal

Table 3.10   Choice board for multiple intelligences

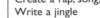

Verbal/Linguistic	**Musical/Rhythmic**	**Visual/Spatial**

Prepare a report
Write a play or essay
Give directions for . . .
Create a poem or recitation
Listen to a tape or
    view a video
Retell in your own words
Create a word web
 	
	Create a rap, song, or ballad
	Write a jingle
	Write a poem
	Select music to enhance a
	    story or event
	Create rhymes that . . .
	
		Create a mural, poster, or drawing
		Illustrate an event
		Draw a diagram
		Design a graphic organizer
		Use color to . . .
		Create a comic strip to show . . .
		Do a storyboard
		Create a collage with meaningful
		    artifacts

Logical/Mathematical		**Bodily/Kinesthetic**

Create a pattern
Describe a sequence
    or process
Develop a rationale
Analyze a situation
Create a sequel
Critically assess
Classify, rank, or compare
Interpret evidence
Design a game to show . . .
 	
	**Free
	Choice**
		Create a role-play
		Construct a model or
		    representation
		Develop a mine
		Create a tableau for . . .
		Manipulate materials to . . .
		Work through a simulation
		Create actions for . . .

Naturalist	**Interpersonal**	**Intrapersonal**

Discover or experiment
Categorize materials or ideas
Look for ideas from nature
Adapt materials to a new use
Connect ideas to nature
Examine materials to make
    generalizations
Label and classify
Draw conclusions based on
    information
Predict . . .
 	
	Work with a partner or group
	Discuss and come to
	    a conclusion
	Solve a problem together
	Survey or interview others
	Dialogue about a topic
	Use cooperative groups
	    to do a group project
	Project a character's point
	    of view
	
		Think about and plan
		Write in a journal
		Keep track of . . . and
		    comment on . . .
		Review or visualize
		    a way to . . .
		Reflect on the character and
		    express his or her feelings
		Image how it would
		    feel if you . . .

Table 3.11   Choice board for a story assignment

Create questions for an interview with a character from the story that questions their feelings or actions	Compose a rap that retells the story	Draw a scene from the story and provide a description of the main conflict
Describe a sequence of events that led to a conclusion	**Free Choice**	Create a role play with dialogue with an alternate solution for the conflict
Bring items or artifacts from home related to the story, and make an oral presentation of their relationships	Work in a cooperative group to create a board game that develops the story	Choose a situation from the story and make a connection to a personal experience that you have had

Table 3.12   Choice board for a book review assignment

Write a book review or trailer of a movie	Write a theme song or ballad for the book	Make a movie poster casting current stars as the lead characters.
Describe a sequence of events that led to a conclusion	**Free Choice**	Act out a favorite part of the book
Where are your characters now? Write the sequel	Interview a character of your choice from the story	Research the author and prepare a report or presentation

approaches to literacy learning—yet relatively few teachers are comfortable enough with visual storytelling to make this an option." Drawing, storyboarding, graphic organizing, and cartooning are very suitable strategies for these learners. Mind mapping is a great tool to idenfity features of a concept, process, or idea or to illustrate the plot or theme of a reading.

DATA COLLECTION

We recognize that it takes time to collect data and to get to know students. We suggest **B.U.I.L.D.** as a reminder to gather information over time as student profiles evolve.

B   **Build over time:** Teachers are constantly 'mining for gold' as they look for student strengths and preferences. It takes time to build the profile and also to move students to self-recognition and reflection.

U   **Use observation:** "Clipboard cruising" throughout the day allows teachers to jot down things that they see to help them know the learner. It may be that the student likes to move around freely or tends to use rhythm or rhyme.

I   **Inventories:** Teachers can collect data from inventories that they ask students to fill in and reflect on. By constructing inventories carefully, teachers can discover many things about students and their learning preferences and needs.

L   **Learner reflection and metacognition:** Teachers can encourage and foster opportunities for student reflection in journals, on tickets out, and with quick writes to get feedback from students about what they have enjoyed, found challenging, or disliked.

D   **Data from a variety of sources:** Teachers collect information from as many sources as possible: from other teachers, other students, parents, and students through inventories, modeling, and demonstrations.

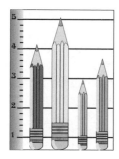

Functional 4
Literacy

Schools have always valued "reading and 'riting and 'rithmetic." These are the foundations for student success. Without functional literacy, students are at a significant disadvantage as learners. We need to make sure that every child in every school develops these skills as early as possible.

FUNCTIONAL LITERACY DEFINED

We define functional literacy as learning to read, write, speak, and listen. Our purpose is to teach students how to read and write to a basic level of functioning by the end of Grade 3 or, for those just learning English, between the third and fifth year of learning the language.

Functional literacy is the foundation that gives students confidence and capability as learners. The ability to read and to write using appropriate conventions is necessary for all students to progress to learning new content and processes throughout their years of formal or informal schooling and lifelong learning. The critical factors in functional literacy include the following:

- Oral language development: speaking and listening
- Phonological awareness: sounds and their differences
- Phonemic awareness: translating sounds into symbols and learning the symbols
- Spelling and early writing: translating symbols into words and writing to convey meaning
- Fluency: rate of reading and flow of sounds, without errors or interference

- Comprehension and meaning: constructing what the written words are about; main ideas; literal information; details noted from words, pictures, speech, and other sources; easily getting the gist of a passage or a graphic
- Narrative and descriptive writing: telling a story, making comparisons and detailed descriptions, other forms of creative writing

ORAL LANGUAGE DEVELOPMENT

In classrooms for many years the modus operandi has been "chalk and talk," with teachers talking and students listening. This is not the most effective way to develop language. Many educational researchers have found that students come to school with too few words in their oral vocabulary (Healy, 1992; Diamond & Hopson, 1998; Levine, 1990). They have spent so many years in front of screens (television and computer) where they have listened (or not) but rarely spoken. This lack of conversation and social interaction has caused a deficit in their vocabulary and oral language. It has also not done much for their attention spans or ability to focus and persevere with a task.

To build trust and develop positive relationships with classmates, students need the opportunity to chat, discuss, debate, and share their thoughts. The ability to express oneself is also a strategy for retention and making meaning, as well as a prewriting strategy. Simple classroom strategies, including Think, Pair, Share (McTighe & Lyman, 1988); Round Table, Round Robin (Kagan 1990); and Inside-Outside Circle (Kagan, 1990), all facilitate dialogue, rehearsal, and oral language development. These strategies are also great for the following types of learners:

- English Language Learners (ELL)
- "Social butterflies" who love to chat
- Students who need dialogue to clarify their thinking and to develop more complex language patterns

Think, Pair, Share

Think, Pair, Share is often suggested to students to use when thinking about an answer to a question or to rehearse their thinking about a topic or concept. The teacher poses the question or ideas and invites students to think about it on their own. Then they turn to a partner and discuss their ideas. Then they should be ready to share with the larger group. When used with questions it gives desired "wait time" so that they are able to access information from long-term memory without feeling rushed or pressured (Rowe, 1987). It takes at least 3 to 5 seconds to access information from long-term memory and bring it back to conscious memory.

Round Table, Round Robin

This is a strategy that monitors participation by having each learner respond or write in turn. Everyone is heard, and students can practice active listening as well as acceptance of others' ideas. It can be used for brainstorming as well as rehearsing, sharing ideas, or giving feedback.

Inside-Outside Circle

This simple tactic is excellent for processing or reviewing information, generating ideas, or problem solving (see Figure 4.1). It is accomplished by forming two circles with the same number of people in each (usually six or seven is a good number). One circle is formed inside the other, and people in each circle face one another. Inside-outside circles provide opportunities for dialogue, social interaction, and physical movement.

People in the inside circle may be asked to share their response to a particular question with the students opposite them in the outside circle, and then students reverse roles. Another scenario might be that each student needs ideas, suggestions, or a critique for their writing, or as a review students can create questions that can be asked to their partners. It is useful for developing vocabulary, practicing dialogue, and spelling words. The most effective implementation is to have the outside circle rotate so that everyone has a new partner, and the same question may be posed.

Figure 4.1 Inside-outside circle

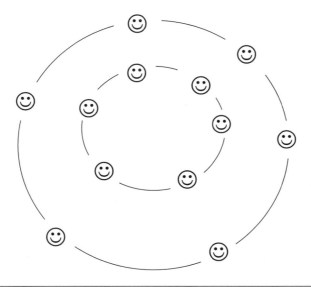

PHONOLOGICAL AWARENESS

Phonological awareness refers to auditory recognition of the sounds and the ability to distinguish between them. With preschoolers, we often play the game I Spy: "I spy with my little eye something that begins with 'P.'" This is often done to soak up time on a road trip and avoid the question, Are we there yet? A two-year-old can often identify the "golden arches" as a favorite place to eat and make the *mmmmm* sound that means "delicious."

Jennifer came home from kindergarten one day with a handout that had twelve pictures on it. Under each picture, she had been asked to write the beginning letter. She had done so correctly, but her mother noticed that all the pictures were scribbled with yellow crayon. When her mother asked about the quality of the work, Jennifer replied that the sounds were important but the coloring was "just because I finished quickly." For Jennifer, there were more important things to do than color between the lines.

How much more interesting and creative would it have been for Jennifer to do the following:

- Draw pictures of her own and give the beginning consonant
- Use magazines or catalogues to find items that began with the same twelve consonants on her handout
- Begin her own sound booklet with a page for each beginning consonant that she knew and perhaps add pictures or words that began with that letter
- Find things in the room that begin with those consonants
- Use anagram cards or blocks to label items in the room
- Make objects out of modeling clay that begin with the consonants
- Use a four-corner graphic to organize beginning sounds, words, and illustrations (see Figure 4.2)

Students don't always have to be working with paper and pencil to be learning. Robert Sylwester (1995) cautions us that we should not restrict and reduce student movement only to handwriting on the limited space of a piece of paper. If we do that, then we neglect the importance of motor development and movement in the learning process.

PHONEMIC AWARENESS

Phonemic awareness is the process of translating sounds into symbols and learning to recognize those symbols and their combinations in words as a beginning step to reading and writing. The stages of phonemic awareness include rhymes, rhythms, symbols, and patterns.

Figure 4.2   Four-corner organizer for kindergarten phonics

Kindergarten Phonics

Beginning Sounds: _____

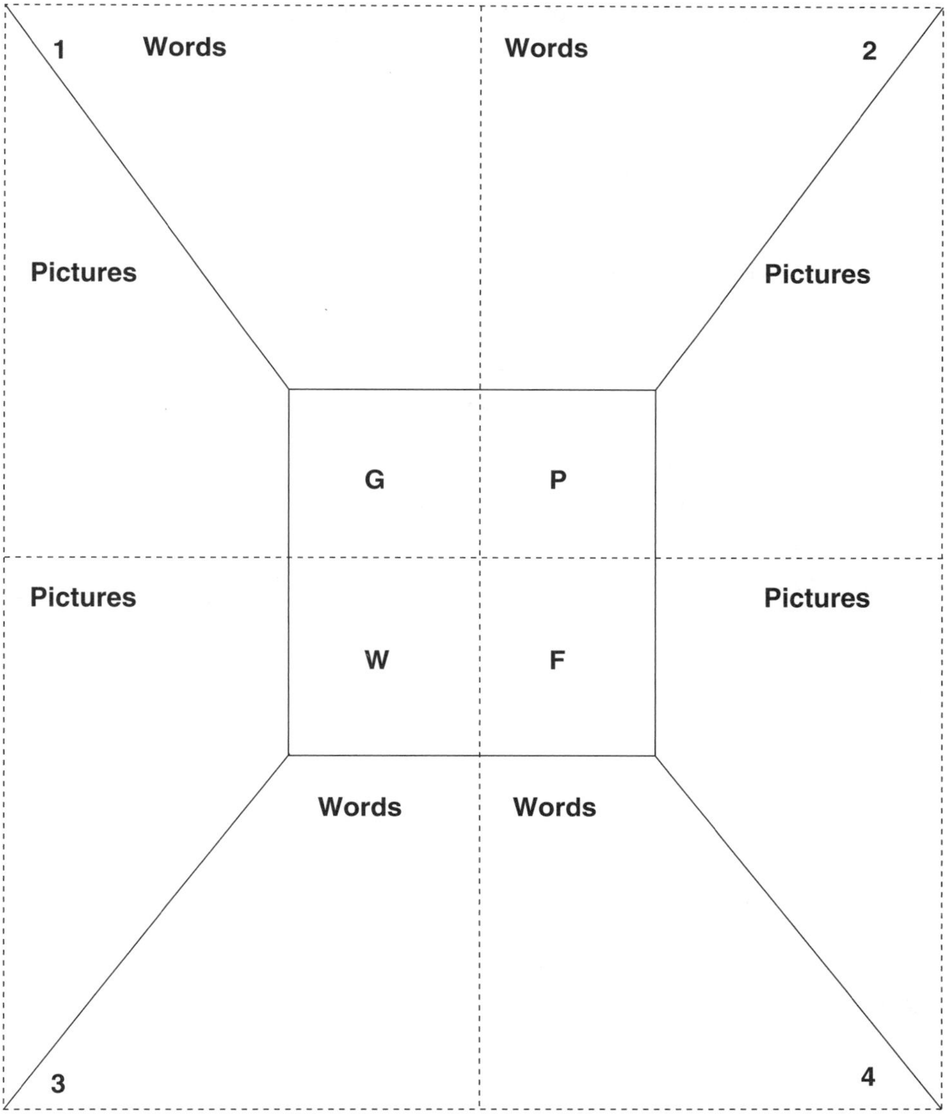

1 **Words**	**Words** 2
Pictures	**Pictures**
G	**P**
Pictures	**Pictures**
W	**F**
Words	**Words**
3	4

Rhymes and Rhythms

Young children enjoy engaging in rhyme and rhythm with words. They enjoy chants and singsong poems. They rhyme word families such as can, ran, man, Stan, Fran, and fan. This is their phonological awareness in practice.

One teacher we know used songs to help students with rhyming words. She sang the first three lines of the song and then left out the last word of the fourth line. The children had to chant the last rhyming word together. As students got the idea, they were even able to provide the third and fourth lines themselves.

> My sister hates to wear her shoes
> I saw her take them off
> She threw them in a **lake**
> Went home to **bake** a **cake**
> My sister hates to wear her shoes
> I saw her take them off
> She threw them in the **trash**
> Now she needs some **cash**
> My sister hates to wear her shoes
> I saw her take them off
> She threw them under the **bed**
> They hit the cat on the **head**
> My sister hates to wear her shoes
> I saw her take them off
> She threw them over the **car**
> Didn't know she could throw so **far**

Using stories, chants, and rhyme gives children the opportunity to recognize rhyming words and create other scenarios or verses of their own once the pattern has been established.

Symbols

As emerging writers, young children begin to scribble and make marks to symbolize ideas and language. They read books through the pictures and realize that the cryptic words are carrying the message (Snow, Burns, & Griffin, 1998).

Patterns

With repetition children seem to be able to "read" a story even when they are not connecting with the written words. They enjoy familiar patterns and predictable story lines such as "Once upon a time . . ." Because children are generally read to, they don't necessarily have a concept for silent reading, and they may believe that written words must be spoken.

Children who grow up in a home where adults have read to them and where reading is enjoyed and valued develop phonological and phonemic awareness more easily and naturally. In print-deprived environments, on the other hand, students do not develop brains with early patterns connected for letter and word sounds. This inability may also result from children who have had untreated ear infections or other problems that affect their hearing and their ability to differentiate sound patterns.

It is not possible for teachers to build on a foundation that does not exist. When students come from poverty or homes where English is not the native language, then teachers will have to work more vigorously with phonics instruction to bring student levels of recognition to a higher point. Thus differentiating instruction and activities is necessary because some learners have solid backgrounds, whereas others are at various stages of phonological and phonemic awareness. Differentiating phonemic activities is crucial to learning to read; the awareness that the child brings to school is one of the greatest influences on their reading success (Adams, 1990; Stanovich, 1986; Snow et al., 1998). Between 40 and 75 percent of young children with early language impairments have reading problems when they come to school (Aram & Hall, 1989; Brashir & Scavuzzo, 1992).

The ability to attend also has a lot to do with the ability to learn to read. Children with attention deficits may not want to pay attention to tasks that are too demoralizing or seem too difficult to achieve. Children tend not to persevere when learning is not a satisfying process. Teachers may want to use the eight multiple intelligences to help children develop their phonemic awareness (see Table 4.1).

SPELLING AND EARLY WRITING

There have been countless books written about spelling and all the ins and outs of teaching it. Some age-old, primitive practices are still alive and well today even though we know they are not effective and are really only busywork:

- Writing the words five times on Monday
- Using them in a sentence on Tuesday
- Writing them in syllables on Wednesday
- Writing the test on Friday

This is not the only way to teach children how to spell. Teachers need to use a variety of strategies to teach spelling and early writing. Students need to have help with the following:

- Spelling strategies
- Daily writing and reading
- Breaking words into syllables
- Using a word wall

Table 4.1 Using multiple intelligences to develop phonemic awareness

Verbal Linguistic	Alphabet books	Students create a booklet with consonants or blends and add pictures or words
	I went to the zoo	Students say I went to the zoo and saw a *bear* not a *bulrush*
	party farm ballgame	I went to the farm and saw a *cow* not a *crane* I went to the beach and took a *towel* The next student must take something that begins with *I*
	Name game	The vintage song "Name Game" . . . Banana Fana . . .
Musical Rhythmic	Clap, snap, or stamp the syllables	Read aloud with rhyme and rhythms in songs, jingles, and poems Use rhymes to help remember the rules "When two vowels go walking, the first one does the talking"
Visual Spatial	Create visual pictures of sounds	Cut and paste from magazines and catalogues of items with initial consonants, and create a scrapbook
Bodily Kinesthetic	Make letters	Create mime and sing songs similar to the song YMCA, where letters are spelled out with the body
Logical Mathematical	Sort letters	Using magnets, cut-out paper, or felt letters, have students match the consonants or blends with pictures or objects
Naturalist	Out in the woods On the beach	Take a visualized or actual walk and have students find as many things that begin with certain letters or sounds
Interpersonal	Buddy sounds	"Say and switch" is a way partners can listen and offer words that begin the same, end the same, or are part of the same word family
Intrapersonal	Things in my room	Students can use their journal to write about word families, rhyming words, and words that start or end with the same sounds

- Using their own spelling booklet (high-frequency words)
- Using the dictionary
- Using spelling rules and generalities

From Invented Spelling to Correct Spelling

With emerging readers and writers, "invented" spelling is often used to encourage writing even if students do not know how to spell the words.

This strategy helps students to write more easily and fluently without worrying about conventions. Using invented spelling can be somewhat risky, however, as many students may see no need to move to more accuracy if not encouraged to do so. To get past invented spelling, the teacher can ask students to write down an initial consonant during reading, and then the teacher, volunteer, or more capable peer editor can write the full word. This models accuracy and imprints the correct spelling of the word rather than imprinting the invented spelling.

It is discouraging for teachers and students to still see invented spelling in middle school. We need to help students think about the strategies they have to get the correct spelling. By constantly exposing students to working with letters and building words, students may become more familiar with patterns and feel more confident with spelling.

Building Words

Students need opportunities to play with letters and create words and understandings of their own. For example, a new vocabulary word such as *teacher* can be transferred to cards or anagrams so that the student can manipulate its letters to form as many new one-, two-, three-, four-, or five-letter words as possible (see Table 4.2). Another strategy might be to have students use a four-squared placemat to go deeper into understanding how a word is formed, what it means, and any rules that apply to its use (see Table 4.3). To help the process and reinforce spelling, the teacher can also tap into the eight multiple intelligences (see Table 4.4).

Table 4.2   Building words through play and creativity

Word: *Teacher*				
I	2	3	4	5
a	he	the	here	reach
	ah	eat	hear	teach
		art	each	cheer
		cat	chat	cheat
		hat	heat	
		ate	tear	
		her		

Table 4.3   Four-squared placemat for building words

Write the word and box it	Draw a picture to help you remember the word
Helicopter	
Break it into parts (syllables) **Write something about the helicopter**	**What rules will help you remember how to spell it?**

Table 4.4   Using multiple intelligences for spelling

Verbal/Linguistic	Verbalizing the sounds of the words in an exaggerated way so that the spelling of the word is clearer. For example, *asparagus* can be said as *as par a gus*.
Musical/Rhythmic	Students create word family booklets with rhyming word families. Beat out or chant the syllables of the word (i.e., *Miss iss ipp i*).
Visual/Spatial	Shut your eyes and see the word. Describe it. Notice the double *I*'s, etc.
Bodily/Kinesthetic	Create a shape out of the word by writing it and adding a line around it. Act out the meaning of the word.
Logical/ Mathematical	Apply any rules that help you remember how to spell the word.
Naturalist	Think about classification: word families, derivations, and origins. Where did the word come from?
Interpersonal	Discuss and work with a partner to help each other remember the spelling.
Intrapersonal	Make notes in your journal with strategies you learned to remember spelling tricks.

FLUENCY

Fluency is the "neglected" portion of functional literacy. Fluency is all about activating our brains to remember words and retrieve them without effort. Students who have problems with fluency display the following characteristics:

- Avoidance
- Fear
- Isolation
- Practicing of errors

Many elementary teachers learn about building sight word fluency through the use of readers that are at the independent, instructional, or frustration level for a student. We are taught to avoid the frustration level. We frequently and mistakenly give students material that is at the instructional level to build fluency. Research has shown that we need to utilize materials at an independent or easy level to build fluency rapidly. Instructional level materials are great for teaching phonics but not necessary for rapid fluency building.

Choosing Curriculum Materials That Promote Fluency

Criteria to guide selection of materials for enhancing fluency are as follows (Gunning, 1998, p. 202):

- Students should be able to read 85 words per minute before moving on to the next challenge
- If students reads 85 words per minute with two or fewer errors, the material is too easy
- It takes the student more than 2 minutes to read a 50 to 100 word passage with more than five errors, the material is too hard

Gunning also found that books for building fluency should contain 75% words that were already taught as part of the phonics instruction and 15% to 20% high-frequency or story words. The functional literacy target is 140 words in one minute—students usually hit this in middle school. For mid-year and end-of-year target rates for reading fluency (Marston & Magnusseon, 1988), see Table 4.5.

California Department of Education's 2001 Criteria for Language Arts Materials Adoption gives us an interesting list that clearly supports fluency. The selected materials must provide support for teachers and students to achieve the following:

Table 4.5   Target rates for reading fluency

Target rates for reading fluency in words correct per minute. Total words read minus the errors equals the words read correctly per minute. Use carefully selected leveled text and short, leveled passages.

Grade	Mid-year	End of year
1	52	71
2	73	82
3	107	115
4	115	118
5	129	134
6*	120	131

*The lower scores at the sixth-grade level compared to the fifth-grade level are attributed to the increased difficulty in sixth-grade material; this sometimes hits at seventh grade depending on the rigor or lack of rigor in the sixth-grade curriculum.

Source: For a fuller discussion, see Marston and Magnusseon (1988).

- Read aloud at the same time (neurological implant)
- Do cross-age reading or reading with an adult who can carefully prompt and correct after the teacher has taught the words
- Tape record your reading and read along with your tape recording
- Use the "I'll read it and you read it" method
- Contain take-home books correlated with learned words
- Templates and materials to make lists of books read—for motivation and earn a book to take home or a magazine (interest specific)
- Turn-taking, plays, radio, learn-your-part strategies

Choosing Instructional Strategies That Promote Fluency

Fluency cannot be taught through word recognition, vocabulary instruction, and comprehension lessons. Fluency is a result of instruction coupled with the opportunity to read the right level materials frequently. You cannot become fluent through instruction, only through reading (Richards, 2000).

Teaching and learning strategies that focus on fluency are an essential part of the elementary teacher's toolkit. The following proven methods promote the acquisition of fluency:

- Modeling (Allington, 1983)
- Repeated readings (Dowhower, 1989)

- ○ Whole group activity
- ○ Independent practice—after guided practice
- ○ Shared readings (combines modeling with independent reading, uses big books paired with student copies of the same text)
- Paired oral reading (Zutell & Rasinski, 1991)
- Oral Recitation Lesson (ORL) uses comprehension clues to prompt fluency like sequences, pictures, and predictions (Richards, 2000)
- Choral reading (Miccinati, 1985)
- Natural language pattern, using materials with repeated language patterns like rhymes, repeating refrains, repeated sentence patterns, predictable text (Hoffman & Isaacs, 1991)
- Readers' Theatre, where students perform a play, poem, or story of some type (Martinez, Roser, & Strecker, 1999)
- Using series books to motivate students who like following a story or genre (Mackey, 1990)
- Using nonfiction thematic materials (Snow et al., 1998)
- Tape assisted reading—students follow and then read along with an audiotape of the text without any background noise or music (Armbuster, Lehr, & Osborn, 2001)
- Reading orally with the child into their left ear helps increase fluency (Henkelman, 1969), even with only a few minutes per day.

Silent Reading Fluency

There is a difference between oral reading fluency and silent reading fluency. Fluent silent reading is the accepted goal of instruction (Stayter & Allington, 1991), but we know that many young children need to hear themselves read: "No research evidence is available currently to confirm that instructional time spent on silent, independent reading with minimal guidance and feedback improves reading fluency and overall reading achievement" (Armbuster et al., 2001, p. 25).

Acquisition of Fluency for Diverse Learners

Students who read orally, as they receive specific guidance, tend to increase fluency rapidly. Traditional round-robin methods don't work very well for many subgroups. Research findings indicate that the instructional methods described above for promoting fluency have greater success.

At least four rereadings are required for a student who speaks standard English and has no disability. More repetitions may be necessary for other students (Armbuster et al., 2001). We need to emphasize that *silent reading of repeated errors does more harm than good for early readers*, especially English language learners, Casual Registry speakers of English, and students with certain learning, linguistic, or perceptual disabilities. Direct instruction is essential to building fluency, especially in these populations.

Teachers need to take strong actions when the following situations become apparent:

- Students have 10% or more word errors in a short passage in one minute
- Students read without expected expression
- Students cannot comprehend what they read

These students need a carefully crafted program to develop fluency.

Students who can orally read 90 words per minute without error usually do not struggle with initial comprehension at the level of the text. Using word cards and having students say the words quickly does not necessarily transfer to text, especially for higher risk students. Choose engaging text over word cards whenever possible. Word calling in isolation has little current research basis (Armbuster et al., 2001).

Good readers who comprehend are fluent readers. Without a level of fluency, comprehension is compromised. Nathan and Stanovich (1991) tell us that researched connection between fluency and comprehension is clear (p. 176). Fluency comprises some distinct characteristics beyond simple recognition of words. In addition to phonemics, Zutell and Rasinski (1991) suggest that fluent readers must be able to do the following:

- Be competent in word recognition
- Read at a suitable rate
- Understand how to project the phrasing and expression of the spoken word upon the written word

LITERACY STRATEGIES FOR DIVERSE LEARNERS

English Language Learners

There some things about English that folks who speak other languages find particularly maddening. To a student learning English, these little quirks make learning this language challenging (see Table 4.6). For some English Language Learners (ELLs), prepositions are a problem along with negatives, the direction of letters, and even the actual formation of letters, words, and sounds.

Learning a new language can be very difficult. So what can teachers do? Only certain specialized teachers are trained to handle English acquisition issues and may even hold degrees and licenses in this growing area.

What about the average teacher in a classroom? Table 4.7 offers a few tips and strategies that may help students in your classroom feel more accepted and learn English a little more easily. Do not let students practice errors either in speaking or writing. Correct students privately and respectfully, just as you would want if you were brave enough to go to school in a different country with a different language.

Table 4.6 The funny things about English

1. English punctuation differs from other languages.
   Examples: Other languages use inverted questions marks and commas, dots in a series, vertical lines, circles, and other markings.

2. There are differences in capitalization.
   Examples: In Serbo-Croatian and Vietnamese, the second word of a geographical place name is not capitalized (e.g., Mississippi river). Cantonese does not use any capital letters to indicate a proper noun. In Spanish, Romanian, Russian, and Portuguese, nationalities are not capitalized.

3. English nouns are not gendered.
   Example: In Spanish, house is a feminine noun.

4. Word order may be different from the subject-verb-object pattern in English.
   Examples: Japanese and Korean are subject-object-verb languages. Arabic is a verb-subject-object language.

5. Plurals may be formed in other ways such as context clues in sentences or by adding something like a word or syllable to a sentence.
   Examples: The Chinese and Vietnamese do not even use plurals, these languages use context clues. Romance languages like Spanish, Italian, and French do use plural forms of words.

6. Pronouns do not have to agree with number or gender.
   Examples: Korean pronouns do not denote gender. The pronoun is sometimes omitted by Spanish speakers because the gender of the person referred to by the verb is handled by the ending to that verb.

7. There are numerous differences in inflection and pacing as well as nonverbal communication.
   Examples: In some cultures, downcast eyes are a form of respect for authority or age, whereas among English language speakers this is seen as disrespectful or inattentive. English language speakers do not emphasize small words like "do" and may cause new English speakers to miss words or sounds.

8. Not all languages contain the sounds in English.
   Examples: The Cantonese speaker does not have experience with the s sound. The French do not have a sound for w. The Vietnamese do not utilize some short vowel sounds like i and a in addition to combinations like ow and ir.

9. English spelling has many irregular forms.
   Examples: Spanish and Vietnamese have spelling forms that match sounds directly.

Table 4.7   Strategies for helping English language learners develop fluency

New Learning	Suggested Strategy
Early learning of nouns and key words	Use pictures and words together
Understanding English dialects	Point out informal patterns, help students to match the correct form to the purpose at hand.
Learning nouns and adjectives	Provide and create pictures. Writing descriptions and short expository pieces like newspaper articles helps.
Learning about the complex use of English pronouns	Read personal narratives and highlight pronouns. Write a letter to a friend. Write about themselves or their families.
Learning root words	Not all languages have root words and word parts: These may have to be highlighted. Use a computer to make bold some of these root words in a reading selection. Underline roots in short written pieces.
When students know very little English	Use picture clues, speak clearly but not louder, use appropriate gestures and facial expressions paired with simple sentences, single words, or noncomplex phrases.
When students are confused by idioms and expressions	Substitute known words; use examples or picture clues. For example, *used to* is an idiom that means "accustomed to or familiar with something."
Early learning of object names	Highlight key words in your classroom with pictures or objects. Label things around the classroom.
Avoiding negative feelings	Learn to carefully pronounce the student's name correctly. Make certain they are not left alone, and make certain students feel welcome in your classroom. Negative feelings on the part of the teacher require no translation.
What is the English level of your student?	Most districts have specialized personnel who can give you this information initially. Remember, many new English speakers understand before they risk speaking and trying to pronounce complex English words.

The Gender Gap

In 1996 The National Assessment of Education Progress indicated that females outperform males by 25 points on a 500-point scale that measures literacy. In comparison with 1992 results, the gap is widening between the genders.

When boys discuss school-based literacy tasks versus things they like to do at home that would be considered literacy based, they use different words and tones (Smith & Wilhelm, 2002). So what will it take to close the gap for boys and change their attitude toward school-based literacy acquisition? First, we must connect males to what they are learning through careful selection of materials, choice, and the establishment of relevance and applicability (Harvey & Goudvis, 2000). Social issues also increase engagement for learners. Boys need opportunities to work in interest groups via literature and information circles. They also often respond to partner reading and writing with concerned mentors.

The following list represents some of the strategies they are using to address the problem in schools and districts where the gender gap is closing (Smith & Wilhelm, 2002; Harvey & Goudvis, 2000):

- Using nontraditional text sources
- Using student interest surveys to help students select text and materials
- Using prereading, reading, and post-reading activities that are hands-on
- Making a clear connection with background knowledge of students
- Using materials that were compelling or address issues to which students can relate
- Answering critical questions versus assigning blocks of text (e.g., "read pages 2–57")
- Preparing for a debate or report on a self-selected topic, which results in less resistance
- Using original source documents that relate to current or future choices and issues
- Clearly establishing purpose
- Good mixing of nonfiction; too much story-based fiction causes resistance
- Selecting choices for action-oriented fiction
- Using multimedia materials or computer-based instruction to augment the text
- Reading aloud to students; this engages them in the materials, and they then want to continue to read more for themselves

These types of instructional strategies and decisions are good for many reluctant learners, not just males. Most adults also prefer purposeful activities and meaningful results.

FLEXIBLE GROUPING STRATEGIES FOR FUNCTIONAL LITERACY

T. A. P. S.

We use T. A. P. S. as a useful term for grouping strategies:

(T) Total group: There may be information and new skills that need to be shared or demonstrated to the whole class.

(A) Alone: Sometimes students need to practice by working alone as they will on standardized tests. In life we often work and think independently of others.

(P) Partners: Partnering gives students a narrow audience with whom to share ideas, discuss new information, or process learning. They may be random partners or teacher-constructed dyads.

(S) Small groups: There are many ways of forming small groups. Groups of three or four students may be constructed for a variety of purposes. Any group larger than three or four has the potential for some students to become off-task or to lack real commitment to the goal.

Here are several types of grouping that can be used with T. A. P. S.:

- Ability: usually homogeneous, based on needs
- Heterogeneous: cooperative group learning
- Random: just to group quickly
- Structured: based on students' profiles and complementary strengths and needs
- Interests: responding to choices and tasks that connect with the learner or pique their curiosity

Table 4.8 suggests a variety of reading and writing strategies for each of the four types of groups whether Total group, Alone, Partners, or Small groups. For a balanced reading program using T. A. P. S., we recommend the following:

T: reading aloud, shared reading
A: independent reading, Drop Everything and Read (D.E.A.R.)
P: buddy, peer, shared reading
S: guided reading, literature and information circles

Total Group: Reading Aloud

Reading aloud may be used one-on-one, to a small group, or to the total group. It is a strategy that promotes active listening, enhances

Table 4.8   T. A. P. S. strategies for reading, writing, speaking, and listening

	Reading	Writing	Listening/Speaking
Total Whole class instruction All students doing the same thing	Modeling new skills Using a jigsaw strategy Text book(s) assignment Guided whole class reading Choral reading	Modeling new skills Brainstorming Word wall building Note taking Using graphic organizers	Read aloud Class discussion Video viewing and discussion
Alone All students working alone may have a variety of tasks based on interest or readiness	Preassessment Choice for individual reading Self-directed reading D.E.A.R.: Drop Everything and Read Reflective reading Retell, relate, reflect	Journal and log entries Portfolios and reflections Self-assessment Independent study Note taking and summarizing All types of writing Tickets out Brainstorming Personal letters	Audiotapes Videotapes CD-ROM Recording stories
Partners All students have a partner: random selection (card, color, etc.). Teacher selection: students choose partners, task or interest oriented	Brainstorming Checking homework Checking for understanding Processing information Peer editing Peer evaluation Researching Echo reading Interest in similar topic Planning for homework SQ3R	Peer editing Peer evaluating Revisions Researching Comparisons Graphic organizers	Think-Pair-Share Say and Switch Peer editing Buddy reading Echo reading Paper Pass
Small groups Homogeneous for skill development Heterogeneous for cooperative groups Random or structured by teacher or students Interest or task oriented	Problem solving Round-robin reading Group guided reading Group investigation Prepare debates with reading materials	Group projects Learning centers Cooperative group learning assignments and summarizing Portfolio conferences Group investigation Carousel brainstorming Graffiti brainstorming Round-robin writing Research and investigation Charts	Literature circles Small group discussion Conferences Round-robin reading Problem solving Small group editing Group brainstorming

vocabulary, facilitates comprehension, and instills a love of reading in children. It also models fluency and voice. It doesn't cost a thing, requires very little teacher preparation, and generally intrigues the learners and captures their attention. It sparks interest in a particular genre or author and often creates an opportunity for readers to self-select similar books to read.

Total Group: Shared Reading

Shared reading, as defined by Regie Routman (1991), is any rewarding reading situation where the learner sees text and observes a more experienced reader (most often the teacher) with fluency and expression. It provides support for learners, and each session is a relaxed, social opportunity for enjoyment and appreciation. Shared reading can involve stories, poems, songs, rhymes, chants, or raps. This may be used from the primary to the secondary level in English and foreign languages. Second language learners pick up the rhymes, sight vocabulary, and fluency.

Shared reading offers struggling readers a way to be involved in reading in a nonthreatening situation. It immerses all readers in rich language without concern about their performance and helps strengthen skills and proves enjoyment.

Big Books are often used in the early elementary grades. Poems, chants, or repetitive stories on charts can be used as well.

Guided Reading

Guided reading may be done with the total group or small groups of students. Using a variety of levels of thinking, teachers can develop questions to challenge all students at a variety of levels.

1. Students are given the passage to read (at or just beyond their personal reading level)

2. Teacher introduces the topic in a novel or engaging way
   a. Discussion and questioning to activate prior knowledge
   b. Introduces the title and makes predictions about the story's contents
   c. Shares objectives and purposes

3. Vocabulary words are introduced and the meanings supplied or discovered

4. Divide up the reading into chunks

5. Students read silently and orally

6. Teacher guides and interacts throughout the reading
   a. Check comprehension and meaning
   b. Question at a variety of levels
   c. Predict and reflect

You may want to use the levels of questioning on the Question Starter sheet to adjust questions at the appropriate level (see Table 4.9). Student-led guided reading can also make use of this resource. It might be helpful to photocopy the question starters on a colored sheet of paper and fold it down the middle. This way the teacher or student leading the guided reading may hold the page as a prompt.

Alone: Independent Reading

Independent reading is an integral part of a balanced reading program. Independent reading gives students individual choice of books to read. The amount of time that students spend reading is a great indicator of their future growth as a reader. Students may need guidance in selection, and they may like to read and reread their favorite books. Teachers may also share appropriate authors with parents so that they can influence their children to select quality reading material. Teachers often conference with students to discuss their ideas and thoughts related to their reading.

Some teachers ask students to keep a reading log and journal to chronicle their reading and reflect on their choices: for example, what they enjoyed, were surprised at, or would like to read next. Suggested prompts for journal entries related to independent reading include the following:

- Why did you pick this book?
- How did you find it?
- How did you like the book? What did you like best?
- Would you read another book by this author?
- What was most interesting about the book?
- Was the title a good one? Why or why not?
- What would you change in the story? Why would you do that?

Students may also be asked to create a report about their favorite book, but that doesn't have to be a traditional written book report. Students might do the following instead:

- Create a poster to advertise it
- Make a diorama of the best scene
- Create a radio advertisement
- Write a letter to a friend
- Design a short skit to interest others in your book
- Write a poem to create interest in the book
- Create a postcard with a picture on one side and message on the other

Table 4.9   Question starters for guided reading

QUESTION STARTERS

Level I KNOWLEDGE (Recall):
1. What is the another name for ... ?
2. What happened after ...?
3. Tell me the facts, steps.
4. What were the characteristics of ...?
5. Which is true or false?
6. How many ...?
7. Who was the ...?
8. Tell in your own words.

Level II COMPREHENSION:
1. Why these ideas are similar.
2. In your own words retell the story of ...
3. What do you think could happen ...?
4. How these ideas are different.
5. Explain what happened after?
6. What is an example of ...?
7. Can you provide another way of saying ...?
8. Who was the key or main character ...?

Level III APPLICATION: (applying without understanding is not effective application)
1. What is another example of ...?
2. Show me a way to ...
3. Which one is most like ...?
4. What questions would you ask ...?
5. Which factors would you change ...?
6. Could this have happened in ... Why or why not?
7. How would you organize these ideas?

QUESTION STARTERS

Level IV ANALYSIS:
1. What are the parts of ...?
2. What steps are important in the process of ...?
3. If ... , then ...
4. What other conclusions can you reach about ... that have not been mentioned...?
5. The difference between the fact and a hunch is ...
6. The solution would be to ...
7. What is the relationship between ... and ...?

Level V SYNTHESIS:
1. Can you make a ... to ...?
2. Why not compose a song about ...?
3. Why don't you make your won way of ...?
4. Can you create new and unusual uses for...?
5. Can you suggest ... for...?
6. How would you deal with ...?
7. What could you do that would ...?

Level VI EVALUATION:
1. In your opinion ...
2. What do you think the chances are for ...?
3. What would the best way be for ...?
4. What do you think will happen is ...?
5. What would work best and why do you think so?
6. Which ways are best? worst?
7. Which ideas are most promising for ...?
8. Which is the better bargain, idea, solution?

Source: Copyright © 2002 Corwin Press. Adapted with permission from *Differentiated Instructional Strategies: One Size Doesn't Fit All,* by Gayle H. Gregory and Carolyn Chapman. Thousand Oaks, CA: Corwin Press, 2002. www.corwinpress.com.

(Adapted from Gregory & Chapman, 2002)

Partners: Paired or Buddy Reading

This is a valuable technique to use with less able readers. One reader who is more capable reads, and the other who is less competent follows along in the text. It is an enjoyable learning experience for the more able reader and models fluency. Even students who are unable to read the material may still be able to discuss and appreciate the content. It gives access to information to all levels of competency. Students from the same grade or class or students from other grades may "buddy" with younger students. Students can also complete an assignment or project after the reading. Students may find a comfortable place for their reading.

Homogeneous Versus Heterogeneous Reading Groups

As an older method of teaching reading, most of us used homogenous reading groups, and they often carried cute bird or animal names chosen by the students. As the students discovered the ability levels of the groups, however, the Seagulls became known as the struggling or poor readers, and the Eagles became known as the proficient ones. There is not a lot of research that supports the use of homogeneous grouping as a strategy for increased student achievement, and yet this practice is still widely used today.

Actually, there is ample evidence that ability groups do not benefit students as much as heterogeneous groups. Studies show:

- Low ability learners actually perform *worse* when they are placed in homogeneous groupings
- Average ability learners benefit *most* from homogeneous groups
- High ability learners have *limited* growth when they work together (Lou et al., 1996)

However, when it comes to reading groups, most teachers are still using ability groups.

When students are grouped by reading ability, teachers tend to treat these groups differently depending on their expectations of that group. Struggling students tend to be given uninteresting and simplistic reading material, asked low-level questions, and are corrected and interrupted more often. It is not only the reading achievement levels that suffer from homogeneous groups but also the students' psychological well-being. Students in the low ability groups often feel excluded from opportunities that others have and suffer from low self-esteem. The impact of this treatment can be devastating and have a lifelong impact.

Small Heterogeneous Groups: Literature or Information Circles

Literature circles have been successfully used to create opportunities for dialogue and to deepen understanding (Daniels, 1994). They can help focus the learner and create reading with a purpose as well as construction of personal questions about the new information. Students in the circle take on specific roles:

- **Discussion Manager:** prepares questions, keeps the conversation moving, and encourages everyone in the group to be involved in the discussion
- **Vocabulary Manager:** looks for new vocabulary words and provides the meaning, illustrates if possible or provides a diagram, points out spelling, and creates a game to review the vocabulary
- **Illustrator:** chooses a situation or event in the story to illustrate and presents and describes it to the others in the group
- **Connector/Reflector:** this group member tries to find a connection to the story from their own lives or perhaps to another story they have read
- **Wordsworth:** this member looks for "lovely language": language such as metaphor, simile, or alliteration that the author uses to create a mood or feeling or to help the reader understand the meaning through feelings or emotions

Although we can explain the roles to students in advance, they may forget or not know what their responsibility is during the complexity of the actual group work. We suggest giving them a bookmark with their role clearly defined as a way to help them focus and lower the stress that the role may carry. The role prompts shown in Table 4.10 can function as bookmarks if they are photocopied and laminated for student use as they participate in the circle.

If students are working in history, science, or another content area, you may want to substitute the name Information Circle. In this case, group roles might be defined in the following ways:

- **Troubleshooter:** helps solve problems in the group
- **Research Conductor:** searches for information that the group needs from a variety of sources, including the Internet
- **Materials Manager:** organizes and collects the equipment and materials for the group
- **Summarizer:** restates the ideas, pulls the discussion together
- **Clarifier:** checks for understanding and clarity of ideas
- **Organizer:** helps the group with sequence of tasks and time

Table 4.10   Role prompts for literature and information circles

Discussion Manager	Vocabulary Manager	Literature/ Information Circles
❖ Make up questions ❖ Keep everyone involved ❖ Direct the discussion ❖ Suggest ideas	❑ Find new words ❑ Look for meanings ❑ Make a picture ❑ Make up a game	

Illustrator	Connector	Wordsworth
➢ Pick a part you like ➢ Make a picture about it ➢ Tell the story with your picture	✓ Find something in the story that reminds you of something in your life ✓ Find something in the story that reminds you of another story	○ Find some words in the story that are "lovely language" It might give you a special feeling or it might just describe something in a special way ○ Examples of simile, metaphor, or alliteration

Small Heterogeneous Groups: Round-Robin Reading

This strategy is effective for students to develop skills in reading, listening, and speaking. It is advantageous for ELL students and works well in heterogeneous groups. A group of four students take numbers, and then each assumes a group role:

1. Person 1 is the reader and reads as much as he or she can.

2. Person 2 is the questioner and creates a question about what has been read.

3. Person 3 is the answerer and answers the question that has been posed.

4. Person 4 is the recorder or supporter and records the question and answer and checks any information or other word meanings (see Table 4.11).

Table 4.11   Round-robin reading

TOPIC: _____

TEXT/PUBLICATION: _____

GROUP MEMBERS: _____

Reader #1: _____	Reader #2: _____

2. Questioner:
  Question: _____
  _____
  _____
	3. Questioner:
	  Question: _____
	  _____
	  _____

3. Answerer:
  Answer: _____
	4. Answerer:
	  Answer: _____

4. Recorder/Supporter:	1. Recorder/Supporter:
Reader #3: _____	Reader #4: _____

4. Questioner:
  Question: _____
  _____
  _____
	1. Questioner:
	  Question: _____
	  _____
	  _____

1. Answerer:
  Answer: _____
	2. Answerer:
	  Answer: _____

2. Recorder/Supporter:	3. Recorder/Supporter:

This works well for reading a chapter from a book (either in English or a foreign language) together or reading a textbook chapter in science or social studies.

Graphic Organizers for Critical Thinking

The critical thinking that takes place as the reader analyzes a story and unpacks the author's thinking can be organized on various visuals so that the reader can see an advance or post organizer of the components of the story. We've supplied four different organizers that could be used for this analytical thinking process (see Tables 4.12, 4.13, 4.14, and 4.15). These organizers can also be used as prewriting and thinking tools to map out ideas and language from the story.

Triangle Organizers for Key Points, Connections, and Questions

After students have read a story, a reflection may be encouraged. Triangle organizers (Schwartz & Bone, 1995) can help students identify the key points in the story, personal connections they may make to the story, and questions they may have as a result of having read the story. See Tables 4.16 and 4.17 for a template and sample triangle organizer.

Student Reflection After Reading

After reading, students may want to use the following prompts to create journal entries:

- I learned that . . .
- I was surprised that . . .
- I discovered that . . .
- I was pleased that . . .
- Explain in your own words
- What was easiest for you?
- What was most difficult for you?
- Draw a picture to illustrate
- Where did you get stuck?
- How did you get unstuck?

These may be put in journals or written on Tickets Out. Table 4.18 shows a 3–2–1 organizer for student reflection after reading.

Table 4.12 Delving into the details

Title _____			Date started _____
Author _____			Planning finished _____
I'll tell my story to _____			I'll tell my story to _____

Characters:		
1.	2.	3.
		Setting:

Problem . . .

Possible Solutions . . .		
Solution #1 First . . .	Solution #2 Next . . .	Solution #3 Finally . . .
	But . . .	

Ending or Solution . . .

Table 4.13   Story analysis

Title _____

Author _____

Characters . . .

1.	2.	3.
❑	➢	✓
❑	➢	✓
❑	➢	✓
❑	➢	✓
❑	➢	✓

Setting:

Where?	When?
Problem?	Solution?

Table 4.14   Problems and solutions

Character(s), setting and their problem(s): _____		
Three ways the characters try to solve the problem:		
First . . .	Next . . .	Last . . .
But . . .	Then . . .	And . . .
Solution: Explain how the character(s) were able to solve their problem and why this solution was successful. Explain how your story will end.		

Table 4.15   Building blocks of a story

Title: _____   Name: _____

Author: _____   Date: _____

1. Main characters

2. Describe main character

3. Describe setting

4. State problem

5. Describe first event

6. Describe second event

7. Describe third event

8. Conclusion

Table 4.16   Triangle organizer to analyze key points, connections, and questions

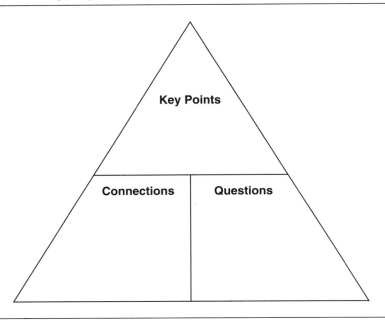

Table 4.17   Triangle organizer as used for story analysis

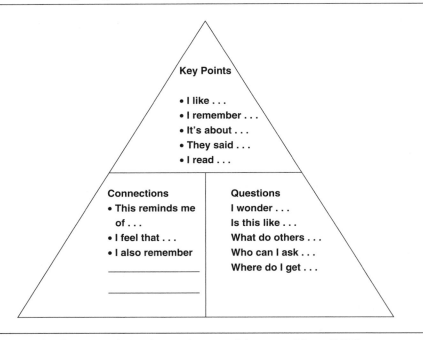

Source: For a fuller discussion of triangle organizers, see Schwartz and Bone (1995)

Table 4.18   3–2–1 organizer for student reflection after reading

3	Things you liked about the story Reasons why _____was your favorite character
2	Connections you made Reasons why this is a good author
1	Idea you had about another story Illustration that caught your attention

FORMS OF WRITING: NARRATIVE AND DESCRIPTIVE

Communication skills include writing and speaking in a variety of forms depending on the situation and need. Table 4.19 outlines four major forms of writing: narrative; descriptive; expository; and persuasive, or influential writing. It summarizes purpose, definition, attributes, and suggested activities for engaging students in each form of writing. We will concentrate on narrative and descriptive writing in this chapter and then discuss expository and persuasive writing in Chapter 5 when we discuss content-area literacy.

To become good writers, all students (regardless of gender, culture, socioeconomic backgrounds) need the following:

- Regular chunks of time each day to write
- A choice of topics that are relevant to the writer
- A response to their writing (teacher, peer, or self-reflection)
- Skills of good mechanics and conventions
- To read to continue to develop rich vocabularies
- To feel safe to risk and share their work
- A genuine purpose for writing

Narrative Writing

Narrative writing is the writing of the storyteller. It can be factual or fantastic and may take many forms such as short stories, novels, and plays, which may include historical or science fiction, fairy tales, fables, myths, and legends. Narrative writing includes the students' ability to accomplish the following:

Table 4.19   Four major forms of writing

Narrative Writing	Descriptive Writing	Expository Writing	Persuasive Writing
Purpose: To create fiction, storytelling	**Purpose:** To give detail, color, and imagery	**Purpose:** To provide information	**Purpose:** To influence others
Definitions: • Tells about the plot, characters, setting, and situations • Includes who, what, when, where, and why • Progresses from beginning to conclusion • Includes crisis and situations that require a resolution	**Definitions:** • Uses sensory-rich language (visual, auditory, smells, tactile, and language) • Adjectives, adverbs • Conjures up colorful detailed pictures	**Definitions:** • Gives details by using who, what, when, where, and why • Tells step-by-step • Gives directions or tells how-to • Recollections or reflections	**Definitions:** • Makes every effort to convince and change one's mind • Provides an opinion or point of view • Provides evidence to support point of view • May include personal beliefs • Uses persuasive language • Has a target audience • Culminates with an final argument
Have students: Newspaper or journal reporting Fact or fictional story Story books, novels Recount events by media	**Have students:** Poetry, stories, situations Detailed explanations that create exact images Create pictures for the reader	**Have students:** Keep a journal or diary of writing Manuals, recipes, and how-to directions News stories Retelling	**Have students:** A speech to sway an audience An editorial to share beliefs Writing for brochures to influence others Forms Advertisements Attempts to convince

- Weave a plot and theme
- Develop characters and settings
- Sequence events and actions
- Define a problem or dilemma
- Create a solution and conclusion

Any of the organizers shown earlier in Tables 4.12, 4.13, 4.14, and 4.15 can be used as an advance organizer for student authors writing a narrative.

Descriptive Writing

This is the language-come-alive form of writing where students use lush and vivid language to create visual images for the reader when they describe people, places, and things. The vocabulary is selected carefully so that the reader can almost see what the author intends. Students will need to increase their descriptive vocabulary in the following ways:

- Visualizing scenes and characteristics
- Describing verbally and then writing
- Using adverbs and adjectives appropriately
- Recognizing this vocabulary in other authors' work

Who? Where? What? How? Why?

To enrich and extend the students' use of descriptive and colorful language, you may want to try a strategy that uses the prompts of Who? Where? What? How? and Why? For example, the first attempt to write a sentence could look like the following sentence:

The cat had a drink.

As the student applies each prompt, the sentence becomes more vivid and descriptive:

Who?	Toby, the cat, had a drink.
Where?	Toby, the cat, had a drink in the kitchen.
What?	Toby, the cat, had a drink of cool water in the kitchen.
How?	Toby, the cat, quickly had a drink of cool water in the kitchen.
Why?	Toby, the cat, quickly had a drink of cool water in the kitchen, as it was a very hot day.

Total Group Writing

Language experience is strategy that builds on students' personal experiences, helps develop personal vocabulary, and helps students see the integration of oral, written, and read language. Chart paper is most often used because it allows the story to be displayed for the group as it is being written and read, and it is used afterward for future reading. Young children love to share their own ideas in story form. The teacher writes the exact language offered and models punctuation and other conventions. Students read their own words in print. These words become a permanent record of events and personal experiences that students enjoy reading again and again. It also models the fact that writers write about things that are important to them in their world, and we all "have a story in us."

Teachers can also write experience charts of their own in front of the students. They can share experiences and model thinking, writing conventions, spelling, handwriting, and vocabulary development. This can be done on chart paper, blackboard, overhead, or whiteboard. It models teacher as writer and integrates the thinking in which writers engage as they write. The teacher talks aloud his or her thinking about content, conventions, vocabulary, and structure.

Alone: Independent Writing

As writers write independently they develop the habit of writing. Writing becomes more fluent, personal, and enjoyable over time with practice. It should be a rewarding, challenging process. It may include all types of writing: narrative, expository, descriptive, and persuasive. It is a thinking process that helps students sort out information, ideas, evidence, and personal points of view. It is also a powerful reflective tool and aids in metacognition and communication of one's thoughts and feelings.

Pairs: Peer Editing

Although students may write independently, they may want to have a peer help them edit their work. This gives them initial and ongoing feedback about the quality of ideas, vocabulary, and conventions they have used in their writing. This dialogue helps the writer rethink their writing process and correct or modify their work well before the final draft.

Pairs: Shared Writing

This is a process that two writers engage in together. It may be teacher and student, student and student, or parent and student. In this coaching situation the pair writes collaboratively with one being more expert and the other more novice writer. They discuss ideas and vocabulary and write together. This shared task builds synergy and confidence as students feel they are not in the situation alone. Various types of writing may be used, such as narrative, stories, recounts, poems, letters, essays, and reports. This is a very supportive writing situation for ELL students and struggling writers. Writers who have trouble with ideas and need coaching and support thrive in shared writing situations. It also lowers the stress of writing independently and appeals to interpersonal learners.

Small Groups: Guided Writing

Guided writing can take place with the whole class, alone, or in small groups. The student is the writer and uses the pencil, pen, or word processor, but the teacher or expert (e.g., parent, paraprofessional, volunteer, more capable student) guides the process and probes such things as the writer's thinking, suitable vocabulary choices, sequence, and conventions. Ultimately we want to enable all writers to be able to write independently, where the coaching and guidance will be through reflection and metacognition.

A BALANCED LITERACY PROGRAM FOR FUNCTIONAL LITERACY

Speaking and Listening

Dialogue and discussion are embedded in all of the strategies and activities we've detailed for reading and writing, which provide ample chances for speaking and listening in large, small, or paired situations. This is important when reading new material, as students need the oral processing to comprehend what they have read and validate or redirect their thinking. In the writing process students often need time to talk out their thoughts to develop vocabulary and crystallize their ideas. Being able to discuss and verbalize during reading and writing is another way that students can sort out their thinking, elicit suggestions, piggyback on ideas, and relax in the process.

In the K–6 classroom where a two-hour block of time has been designated for language development—reading, writing, listening, and speaking—we recommend that all aspects of the literacy program be included each day. Table 4.20 suggests the time and focus in each block. The times may be adjusted as needed in any classroom. Speaking and listening are embedded in all aspects of the learning process.

Table 4.20   A balanced literacy program for a two-hour block

Large group read-alouds, Independent reading, D.E.A.R., Buddy, Peer, and Shared reading, Guided reading, Round-Robin Literature Circles		Whole group writing, Write-alouds, Guided writing, Independent writing, Shared writing, Peer editing. Various types should be included: narrative, descriptive, expository, persuasive	
	Reading 30 minutes	**Writing** 30 minutes	
Phonics Vocabulary development, Spelling, Grammar Conventions	**Word Study** 30 minutes	**Application** 30 minutes	Centers, Contracts, Projects, Agendas. Analytic, practical, and creative applications

Four-Corner Graphic

Four-corner graphics are versatile visual organizers that students can use for all literacy competencies (see Tables 4.21 and 4.22). They offer models that students can use to record concepts or to develop detailed descriptions of story settings, plots, or characters. Students can brainstorm ideas for each prompt and jot down notes and vocabulary to use later as a reflection for reading or as a resource for writing.

Choice Boards

Using choice boards allows students to develop their abilities and to practice their functional literacy skills. Integrating all different kinds of reading and writing assignments gives students choice and variety and also helps them see how all four literacies and all four forms of writing are necessary for their repertoires.

Choice boards also give the teacher an effective way for respectfully honoring the unique multiple intelligences of all their learners (see Tables 4.23 and 4.24).

We hope this chapter has given you an overview of functional literacy and the many strategies you can use to help all learners build their literacy skills, confidence, and success regardless of background, commonalities, or differences.

Table 4.21   Four-corner organizer for analyzing a story

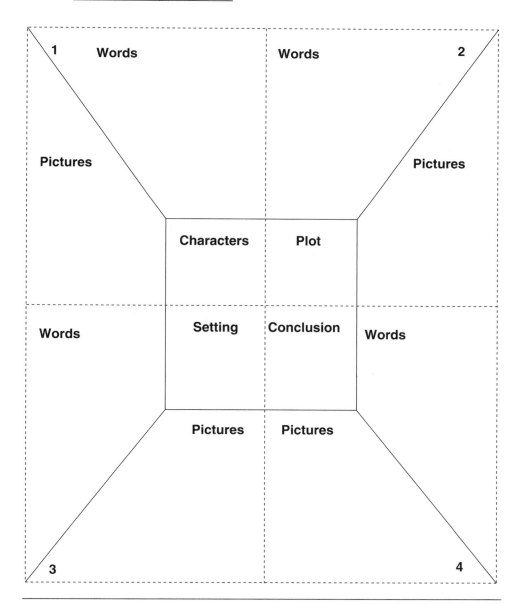

Table 4.22   Four-corner organizer for building a character sketch

Character Sketch

Character: _____

1	2

How she looks	**How she does**
Words she uses	**What she likes**

3	4

Table 4.23 Using choice boards for descriptive writing

Comic Strip	**Vocabulary Squares**	**Fact/Opinion**
Illustrate an important event from the beginning, middle, and end. Write a caption for each picture.	Pick six words from the content word wall, write a sentence, and draw an illustration to demonstrate the meaning of each word.	Write five facts from the story and five opinions about the story. Give them to a partner to sort.
Partner Reading Read a book with your partner by taking turns. Evaluate your fluency and rate your partner's fluency. Use the rubric.	**Free Choice!**	**Character Study** Draw a Venn diagram comparing you with the main character. Use B.O.W. (Brainstorm, Organize, Write) as a guide. Consider appearance, actions, and circumstances.
Analogy Write an analogy. My character is like a _____ . It reminds me of _____ because _____ .	**Connection/Reflection** Write about how this story connects to another story. What is similar, what is different? Use an organizer of your choice to show your thinking.	**Point of View** Write a summary of the story from the point of view of a character of your choice.

Table 4.24 Sample choice boards for young learners

Goldilocks

Rewrite and illustrate a new version of the story *Brown Bear, Brown Bear, What do you see?*	Create a song about bears using the facts that you know.	Compare polar and grizzly bears using the attached organizer.
Interview Goldilocks about what she learned about bears.	**Free Choice!**	Create a mural or diorama of the habitat of the polar or brown bear.
Dramatize or mime hibernation and the preparations involved.	Create a menu for the "Bear Café." Include the foods that both the brown bear and polar bear would prefer.	Create a new ending for the story of *Goldilocks and the Three Bears.*

(Continued)

Table 4.24 (Continued)

Dr. Seuss

Pick a page from your favorite Dr. Seuss book and act it out.	Find and match all the rhyming words.	Create a mural of your favorite part of a Dr. Seuss book.
Interview a character from a Dr. Seuss book.	**Free Choice!**	Survey the class and graph your results (e.g., favorite character).
Create a rap from a Dr. Seuss book.	Read your favorite part to the class from a page of a Dr. Seuss book.	Journal activity: In your opinion, why should other people read this book?

A novel or story

Make a K.W.L. chart of the story.	Pair share, and interview major or minor characters.	Create a mind map to summarize the story.
Create a poster that reflects the main theme or another theme of the story.	Free Choice—create your own activity relating to the story.	Develop a dance or rap of an important event in the story.
Create a story using a Building Block.	Readers' theater. Dramatize a reading from the story.	Develop a script with a change in the ending.

Gingerbread Man

Interview the fox at the end of the story. As a reporter, ask the fox 3–5 questions about what he did.	Using your five senses, describe how a gingerbread man tastes, feels, smells, looks, and sounds when you are eating it.	Role-play a new ending for the story.
Make a time line showing the order of characters he met in his journey.	**Free Choice!**	Make a graph measuring and weighing your gingerbread man compared with that of five other students.
Create a song, poem, or rap about the Gingerbread Man.	Make a gingerbread man. Be as creative as you like with the materials. Examples: clay, dough, construction, paper, food, etc. Describe him in your own words.	Think of a place you would run to if you were the gingerbread man. Write a postcard from this place.

Content Area Literacy 5

Every teacher in every classroom in every school is a literacy teacher. Every discipline has a vocabulary particular to its content. Each discipline uses language to talk about its ideas and concepts, and reading and writing are part of the interactive instruction in that subject area. Each of us is responsible for furthering the literacy standards. Teachers throughout the school need to dialogue about the literacy needs of their students and target developing those skills for their students' growth and achievement.

CONTENT AREA LITERACY DEFINED

We define content area literacy as reading, writing, speaking, and listening to demonstrate content area learning. Our purpose is to understand and use content area-specific knowledge and skills directed toward a specific result or demonstration of skill through a variety of means. The critical factors in content area literacy include the following:

- Vocabulary acquisition: gateway to using content area knowledge, development, and interconnection of concepts in a content area
- Question formulation: to understand and inquire further about a content area skill or concept
- Text orientation: understanding the construction and factors that aid meaning in text or material construction for a particular content area, including graphical or visual representations as well as book parts and text clues
- Expository writing: factual information to recount, inform, or direct a reader. Convey thinking about a content area topic or problem, note patterns or trends, and demonstrate usefulness of the content area

- Presentation and product creation: performance-based summative demonstration of the integration of information and skills for a given topic or problem

VOCABULARY ACQUISITION

Wonderful teachers throughout the world have introduced students to new words today. They use a variety of methods including definitions, sample sentences, speaking and looking at the word, and perhaps writing the word. Tomorrow when students return to class, most will not remember the new words. How frustrating! Let's ask *Why* and *What*:

- Why does this happen?
- What distinguishes a learning experience that results in a student remembering a word from a learning experience that does not lead to remembering?
- More important, what increases the probability that the student will understand the word and be able to communicate effectively with it and about it?

We know so much more now about how students acquire and retain concepts than we used to. We have brain research, English language acquisition research, literacy research, and more. A common theme that runs through these studies has to do with how students learn new concepts, use them, and retain them. Another set of studies concerns the strategies teachers should use to get the desired level of thinking about specific concepts. Vocabulary acquisition is the start of concept attainment and understanding. Vocabulary is also the gateway to the inferential thinking needed for deeper understanding and problem solving in any area or situation (Marzano & Arredondo, 1996). The acquisition of vocabulary impacts our ability to understand what we read and hear. It influences what we say and write to express our thinking. In the absence of excellent vocabulary acquisition strategies, students will not progress as fast, and some students will not be able to access the content they must learn (Armbuster, Lehr, & Osborn, 2001). Vocabulary acquisition strategies are not often systematically taught in methods classes at universities and sometimes do not get enough attention in literacy classes for elementary or specialized teachers.

So, which strategies should we use, under what circumstances, and for which students? We have selected strategies in this chapter that have high payoff for diverse students and work especially well in acquiring content-specific vocabulary. There are certainly other strategies. We chose these because of their applicability to content areas and the ease of using them for all teachers regardless of specialty, grade, or content area. Other chapters in this book point out strategies that are less content dependent, but in this chapter our focus is on content area literacy.

Learning New Words for New Concepts

We now know that vocabulary that is explicitly taught increases the probability of retention and comprehension (Ellis, 1995). The meaning of some new words can be acquired implicitly or through repetition without direct strategies. Take the example of the word *muggle* in the Harry Potter books. Students all over the world in several languages know that a muggle is someone without magic powers. The number of repetitions in the first book of the series and in the context in which it was consistently used helped students retain and understand the word.

This strategy works for some types of single-meaning words for students who are good readers. Young readers who can recognize a novel word from a predictable or high-frequency word have an advantage in acquiring new vocabulary in their primary language and in other languages.

This phenomenon also leads to certain interesting conclusions that have been well researched since the 1970s. Although repeated exposure to a word does help retention, both retention and comprehension are far more likely if a specific cycle takes place (Craik & Lockhart, 1972):

1. First, students notice that a new word is unfamiliar.

2. Then, students use specific strategies to attempt to infer meaning from context (verbal or written).

3. Finally, students are taught strategies that include both repetition and association techniques that are semantic or image based.

Repetition can be used for some simple survival and interpersonal vocabulary, but it is of little use with abstract vocabulary. A combination of strategies that employ both repeated exposure and context are far more effective.

Sternberg (1998) has identified three basic subprocesses for acquiring content or context-based vocabulary. These same principles align with Marzano's (2003) general high-payoff strategies and with Crow and Quigley's (1985) language acquisition strategies. All agree that learning content vocabulary from context requires the following:

1. Separating relevant and nonrelevant information for formulating a definition or rules about the word.

2. Combining text, verbal, and visual clues to develop a working definition.

3. Relating the new word to prior information already stored in our long-term memories (Sternberg, 1998).

Given these three parameters for success, it may be surprising to remember the way that many of us were first taught vocabulary.

1. Look up the word in the dictionary, and write the definition.

2. Use the word in a sentence.

3. Write the new word numerous times.

According to Nagy (2000), however, those are the three least effective ways to teach new vocabulary. In study after study, these common practices failed to increase comprehension (Mezynski, 1983; Gallagher & Pearson, 1989; Stahl & Fairbanks, 1986). So why are they so widely used today? Teachers need to have better tools to meet the needs of diverse learners who clearly acquire vocabulary differently and utilize strategies that promote more rapid retention and comprehension.

Not All Words Are Created Equal

Before helping teachers with these strategies, we need to discuss the density or specificity of words. Not all words are created equal. Some words are important abstract concepts or lead to broad and diverse levels of interpretation. Some words are very specific and have a limited range of interpretation and application. Educators in most classrooms do not distinguish between these types of words. If they do distinguish, they may not pay attention to the strategies they employ to teach different words with different density of meaning and interpretation. Here are three words as examples:

- Freedom
- Citizenship
- Vote

At the elementary level we spend time on *vote* and a little time on *citizenship,* but sometimes we forget to introduce and connect specific vocabulary to the abstract concepts. These important concepts—like *freedom*—are often foundation words for higher-level comprehension in content areas that begin in the elementary grades and then build as the students move toward middle and high school depth of understanding.

Using specific techniques helps our students form connections and distinguish similarities and differences in these dense and complex words. Spending additional time on complex or abstract concepts often gives students an umbrella or organization tool for grouping other words. So, if we teach that citizens in democracies get to vote and that is an important characteristic of the complex idea we call freedom, then students are far more likely to retrieve and understand all three of the words.

We could even more powerfully impact learning by pairing this explanation with a visual cuing system based on hundreds of studies from many countries about what teachers need to consider to promote vocabulary acquisition:

- Think about connections
- Think about relevance
- Think about parts-to-whole relationships
- Think about patterns
- Think about concept attributes and uses

Organizing the strategies that work well requires us to remember three things (Nagy, 2000): integration, repetition, and meaningful use (see Table 5.1).

Choosing Words for Study

Introducing complex concepts in combination with other words that define or clarify the abstract nature of the concept helps students. You can do this by choosing groups of words that have related meanings, words critical to understanding text or specific content materials. You can also group simpler words that have general utility in language.

Teaching words in isolation is a poor strategy, especially without contextual application. Be careful not to introduce words that are too similar in close proximity or in the same 24-hour period. An example is "latitude" and "longitude." They are too similar, and if you introduce them both in the same lesson, you decrease the probability of retention. The brain stores

Table 5.1   Three things to remember about vocabulary acquisition

1. Integration: Knowledge is structured and consists of relationships; we understand information by relating it to what we already know so that we recognize patterns	**Methods that Work:** Visuals or Models Semantic Mapping Semantic Feature Analysis Hierarchical and Linear Arrays Constructivist Approach (construct meaning)
2. Repetition: The human brain uses repetition for forming memories and relationships over time and circumstances	**Methods that Work:** Read, read, read; then speak, listen, and write; then read, read, read!
3. Meaningful Use: Utilizing newly learned ideas and words in a variety of contexts causes learning	**Methods that Work:** Multisensory approaches Questioning Association of Ideas Defending an Idea Side-by-Side Context

memories by similarities but retrieves them by differences. It takes a good night's sleep to create long-term memory pathways. If you separate instruction of similar concepts by at least 24 hours, you will increase the probability that students will be able to form long-term memories and retrieve the information (Sousa, 2003).

In the latitude and longitude example, if you teach one of these words and then follow the next day—with minimal repetition—with an explanation that we can find things more easily in geography by using a second factor or number, you will increase learning. In our earlier example with freedom, citizenship, and vote, same-day learning would work because the words are different in complexity and have a clear associative or hierarchal attribute.

This is the same principle that tells us not to learn to swing a bat and a golf club in the same day; they are too similar for motor memory as well. In the case of elementary students, we should not teach students how to write a cursive p on the same day as g or q because they are too similar. The idea of word families and context is good only if there are distinguishing features in your choice of words. Rhyming words are an exception. These can be taught together because the brain is hardwired to acquire oral language, and it loves patterns. The differences in consonant sounds are sufficient for long-term memory retrieval here (Sousa, 2003).

Developing Independence in Vocabulary Acquisition

What are the skills strong literacy learners use to acquire new words? Students who are provided with the following kinds of strategies have increased success:

- Context skills
- Structural analysis of suffixes
- Visual clues
- Motivational methods
- Dictionary as the "Internet search" to research
- Teach limits of utilizing one method
- Opportunities for reading and reflection across content areas

Vocabulary Acquisition Is the Gateway to Inferential Thinking and Comprehension

Making inferences is a difficult abstract skill, yet it is the foundation of comprehension. It is not found literally in a test. Inferences are logical conclusions based on evidence. They are not opinion and are not influenced by emotion but by concrete facts. Writers don't necessarily tell all but slowly share their information throughout the text. It is a way of allowing the reader to make meaning from background information, personal past experiences, and information shared but not explicitly stated by the author.

Higher-level thinking skills start with good vocabulary instruction. Students who are systematically taught vocabulary in a content area do better on standardized tests. Students who are learning English acquire it more rapidly and accurately. The strategy for acquiring vocabulary must match the purpose or the content, and teachers can choose powerful strategies to help students acquire new words (see Table 5.2). These strategies can be used on their own, but they are also very effective in combination. Some will work better for new teachers; some will work better at different grade levels or times of the year, depending on student developmental needs.

Table 5.2   Vocabulary strategies with high payoff for students

	Key Strategies Across Content Areas
Verbal Rehearsal Craik and Lockhart (1972)	• Check for vocabulary use in discussions, give out word cards, or post words to remind students to use them • Require specific vocabulary use in oral presentations • Use Think-Pair-Share • Connect with prior learning—of what does the word remind you, or what other words are associated with the target word?
Visual Clueing Kuzmich (2003)	• Post key vocabulary words, expect that they will be used in writing during the unit • Write key vocabulary words at the top of papers when requiring short, constructed response items • Can be used with Verbal Rehearsal and other strategies
Examples and Nonexamples Frayer, Frederick, and Klausmeier (1969)	Use the Frayer method or other graphic organizers and have students come up with: examples, nonexamples, a nonlinguistic representation, or a use for the word
Analogies Marzano (2003)	• Connect to prior knowledge • Use opposites • Compare and contrast • Use as prompt questions for discussion • Use verbal, visual, or written analogy-based prompts

(Continued)

Table 5.2 (Continued)

	Key Strategies Across Content Areas
Pictures and Demonstrations Harvey and Goudvis (2000); Kuzmich (2003)	• Use posters • Use pictures on homework • Demonstrate an idea • Have students role-play an idea • Color highlight or underline key vocabulary
Combining Clues to **Utilize the Definition** Ellis, (1995)	• Give clues leading to a definition • Develop characteristics or patterns • Develop relationships to prior knowledge • Have students guess word or concept given its use

Verbal and Physical Memories
 	
Sousa (2003); Kuzmich (2003)
	• Use question starters that are relational:
	    What does it feel like if . . .
	    What does it look like if . . .
	• Verbalize as you perform an action or demonstration
	• Attach a physical movement with the word
	• Type a written response that uses key words

Key Word Method Burke (2002)	• Not all words are equal, so teach the underlying concepts through use in writing, headings to a table or graph, and bold print • Teach technical vocabulary using feature analysis, and relate back to underlying main idea • Always establish parts-to-whole relationships
Creating Patterns and **Graphic Organization** Johnson and Pearson (1984)	• Use Semantic Mapping, Cause and Effect Mapping, and other methods requiring the use of a graphic organizer • Use multiple column note taking • Use hierarchical or linear arrays to show relationships
Semantic Feature Analysis Johnson and Pearson (1984)	• Turn Venn diagrams into feature analyzers • Use charts with words or attributes • Show characteristics of the word or group of words • Show relationships among words

FORMULATING QUESTIONS FOR CRITICAL THINKING

Formulating questions before, during, and after reading and writing is essential for critical thinking. Questioning helps students to convey meaning, voice, and purpose with greater depth and clarity (Paul & Elder, 2001). Elementary students might want to use a checklist like the following for thoughtful writing:

- What is this about?
- Who will read this writing?
- Why should someone read my work?
- What do I want someone to get from my writing?
- Does my writing make sense?
- Do I have details that make my writing easy to understand?
- Do I stay with the idea I started with in my writing?
- Are my facts correct?
- Did I use evidence to help readers understand my writing?
- Did I correct all my errors?
- Would I be proud to share my writing?

Table 5.3 offers another checklist that students can use for self-evaluation of writing.

Critical Thinking

You cannot teach students to think. You can expose them to methods that result in critical thought. The numerous parts of the brain involved in comprehension can be activated through a variety of methods (Sousa, 1995). Emotions play a strong role in thinking and learning, as does crafting learning opportunities that result in positive connections within the brain:

> There is growing evidence that humans are born with a brain that has all the sensory components and neural organization necessary to survive successfully in its environment. . . . Every bit of the evidence available suggests that the human brain is designed for thinking (Sousa, 1995, pp. 111–112).

We can teach students to organize information and to promote efficient and logical thought. However, we must do so systematically and throughout the school day. Similar structures used across content areas and time help the brain use natural connections and patterns. Diverse learners must be taught to observe, find patterns and schema, develop logic in drawing conclusions, extrapolate information, and elaborate ideas (Marzano & Arredondo, 1996).

Table 5.3   Checklist for student self-assessment of writing

Select the face that shows how your writing rates.	☺	😐	☹
Ideas:			
My message is clear	☺	😐	☹
I know enough about my topic	☺	😐	☹
I try to make it interesting	☺	😐	☹
Organization:			
My paper has a good beginning	☺	😐	☹
I tell things in the right order	☺	😐	☹
My paper ends well	☺	😐	☹
Conventions:			
I used paragraphs	☺	😐	☹
It is easy to read my penmanship	☺	😐	☹
I use periods and question marks	☺	😐	☹
I use capital letters correctly	☺	😐	☹
Voice:			
This writing sounds like me	☺	😐	☹
I say what I think and feel	☺	😐	☹
My reader will be interested	☺	😐	☹

Schema: Helping Students Develop a Personal Set of Learning Strategies

Teachers can help students with all of the following:

- Describing the method used to come up with an answer, solution, or process
- Learning multiple ways to solve any problem or dilemma
- Persevering with resilience when they try a strategy, acknowledge it does not get the desired results, and then try another strategy or seek out a new method
- Conveying acceptance and praise for the use of multiple strategies and solutions

- Offering systematic instruction in effective strategies including brainstorming, plus-minus-interesting, T-chart, pros and cons, flow charting, mapping, creating a visual representation, and so forth

Questioning Is the Hallmark of Critical Thinking

Questioning assumptions and questioning your own decision-making are the key factors in content area literacy. Students who can determine purpose, seek clarity, and self-evaluate are students who can question assumptions and detect errors in thinking or process (Paul & Elder, 2001). Many groups of diverse learners have a difficult time self-evaluating and determining cause and effect. Use of graphic organizers, real-life situations, and stories or videos of peers solving problems are good techniques to use with these kinds of learners.

TEXT ORIENTATION

Students are often asked to read a chapter in the textbook. As we recall our own experience at this task as students, many of us may remember *not* remembering what we had read on the previous page. This was especially true if the ideas were new, the vocabulary was vague, and we really didn't have a purpose for reading it. We may have gotten lost in print, or the reading activity may not have done much to create understanding or long-term memory. It is important that students see a purpose for their reading and develop an understanding of the vocabulary for the content. Teachers can find effective strategies to hook learners before reading, engage them during reading, and then enhance their learning after reading (see Table 5.4).

Table 5.4   Strategies for engaging learners before, during, and after reading

Before Reading	During Reading	After Reading
"Hooking"	"Engagement"	"Enhancement"
K.W.L.	Dot, Jot	Learned column
K.I.C.	Highlighting	Prediction checks
K.P.C.	Symbol notations	Finish webs
Concept web	Wonder column	Retells
Mind map	Interest column	Murals, mind maps
Graphic organizers	Graphic organizers	Foreshadow what's next
Graffiti placemat	SQ3R	Summarizing and note taking
Character sketch	Reciprocal teaching	Discussion
Anticipation guides	Literature and information circles	Question swap

K.W.L., K.I.C., and K.P.C.

We know that the brain needs to connect with previous knowledge and look for similarities and differences between past information and new information so that learners can construct their own meaning for new knowledge (see Figure 5.1). K.W.L is a strategy first introduced by Donna Ogle (1986) to help students focus on a topic by connecting with prior knowledge:

- The *K* stands for, what do I *know* or think I know? which opens mental files and pulls out prior knowledge from students' long-term memory.
- The *W* stands for, what do I *want* to know or wonder about? which helps students identify their areas of interest or passion so that teachers can tap into those areas and design learning to capitalize on interests.
- The *L* stands for, what has been *learned?* and facilitates reflection on learning and usefulness of learning.

K.W.L. can be useful as a prereading strategy to help students make sense out of print. It helps students focus on personal information as well as on interests, passions, and curiosity. It also provides a vehicle for making predictions and facilitating critical thinking and reflection. Two variations on K.W.L. are K.I.C. and K.P.C.:

- K.I.C.
  o The *K* stands for what I *know.*
  o The *I* stands for what *interests* me.
  o The *C* stands for *choice:*
    – Who might I like to work with?
    – What might I like to explore in the content?
    – How might I like to show what I learned?

- K.P.C.
  o The *K* stands for what I *know.*
  o The *P* stands for what I *predict.*
  o The *C* stands for *check:*
    – Who could I ask?
    – Where could I look?
    – How was my thinking accurate or inaccurate?

Anticipation Guides

Using anticipation guides (Head & Readence, 1986) before reading also gives students an opportunity to focus on the content in the chapter and open their "mental files" to discuss and review what they already know or think they know. Anticipation guides set up curiosity and anticipation for the learning to come. They can serve as a preassessment to identify what students know (or have misconceptions about) and want to know. Table 5.5 shows an anticipation guide from which students can work before

Figure 5.1 K.W.L., K.I.C., and K.P.C. strategies

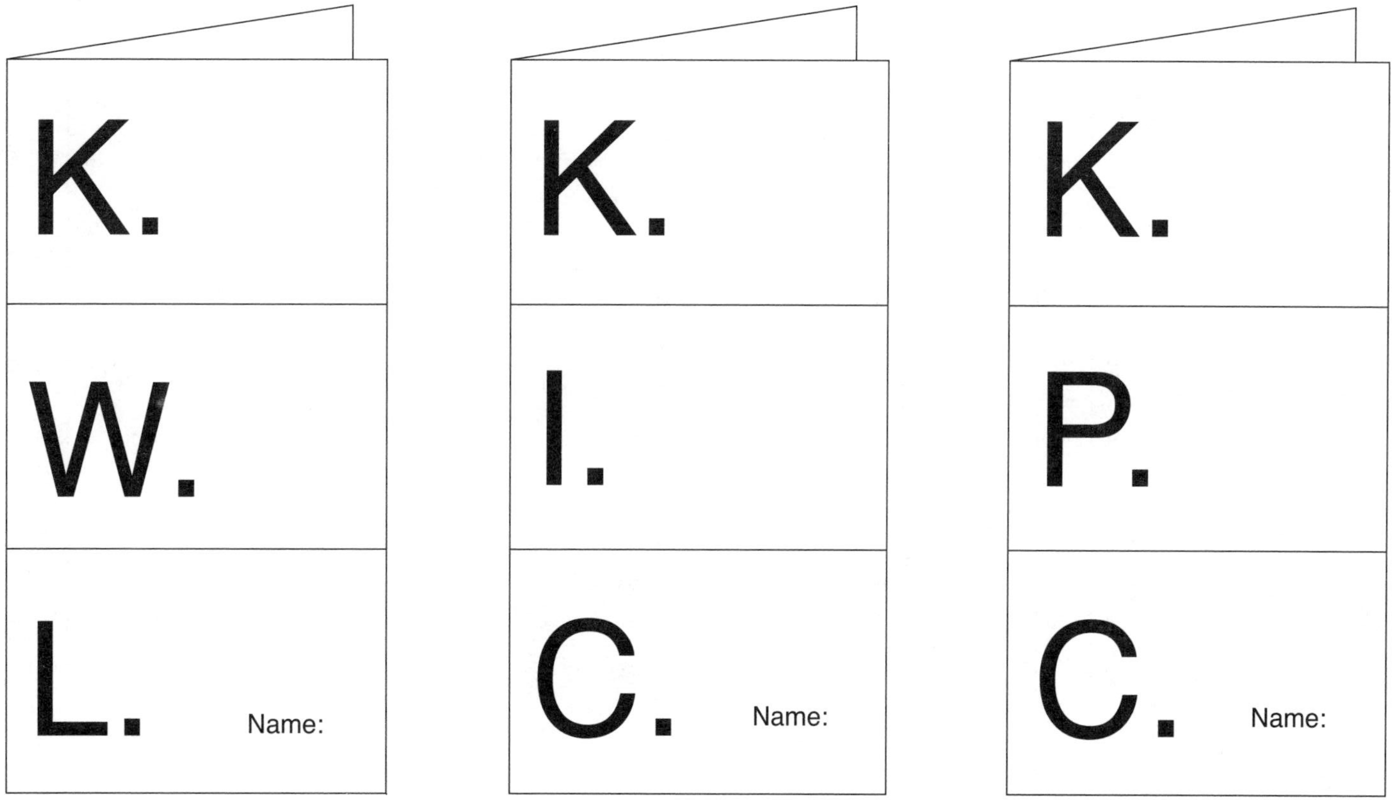

reading a chapter or viewing a video about insects. After reading, the students can revisit the guide to see if they have changed their minds. Table 5.6 offers a reproducible template that teachers can offer students to create anticipation guides for other topics.

Table 5.5   Anticipation guide for reading assignment about insects

Before the reading		Consider these:	After the reading	
Agree	Disagree		Yes	No
		Insects have six legs.		
		All insects can fly.		
		Insects hibernate.		
		Insects are poisonous.		
		All insects lay eggs.		
		All insects eat leaves.		

Table 5.6   Template for anticipation guide

Before the reading		Consider these:	After the reading	
Agree	Disagree		Yes	No

Note Taking and Summarizing

Marzano, Norford, Paynter, Gaddy, and Pickering (2001) offer strong evidence that a key skill for learners is being able to summarize, including picking out key points and deleting extraneous material. Marzano reminds us that note taking and summarizing, as well as providing advance organizers, are effective strategies for increasing student achievement (see also Figure 1.5 in Chapter 1). As students are introduced to a new textbook or a new chapter in a textbook, there are things teachers can do to orient the students and increase the chances that they will succeed in reading for information and comprehension, even though many (if not most) texts are filled with facts that have not been organized in a way that allows students to see the important information and the supporting details.

Students can be given frames for summarizing, for using rules to classify importance of information, for defining concepts, and for creating arguments to support claims.

Summarizing

1. Deleting things

2. Substituting things

3. Keeping things

The Rule-Based Strategy

1. Delete trivial material that is unnecessary to understanding

2. Delete redundant material

3. Substitute superordinate terms for lists (e.g., insects for bee, ants)

4. Select a topic sentence, or invent one if it is missing

The Definition Frame

The purpose of a definition frame is to describe a particular concept and identify subordinate concepts:

1. Term: the subject to be defined

2. Set: the general category to which the term belongs

3. Gross characteristics: those characteristics that separate the term from other elements in the set

4. Minute differences: those different classes of objects that fall directly within or beneath the term

The Argumentation Frame

The argumentation frame contains information designed to support a claim:

1. Evidence: information that leads to a claim
2. Claim: the assertion that something is true; the claim that is the focal point of the argument
3. Support: examples of or explanations for the claim
4. Qualifier: a restriction on the claim or evidence for the claim

The argumentation frame will lead to a persuasive piece of writing.

Highlighting During Reading

Highlighters are wonderful inventions and can make the assigned text look like the reader has made real progress. Sometimes, however, students have just highlighted everything on the page, unable to distinguish between what is important or critical information and what is just nice to know. Teachers may want to work with students when using highlighters, color-coding information for the students using one color for key information or main ideas and a second color for secondary information.

Symbol Notations With Self-Sticking Notes

Coding information is a way to help students make sense out of textbook information and also help them focus and analyze their own comprehension levels (Tompkins, 2003). Teachers can set up codes for different types of responses to information, or students can invent their own codes. They may also jot down why a symbol was used, what questions they have, why the information is interesting, and so forth (see Figure 5.2).

Figure 5.2   Sample symbols and codes for comprehension

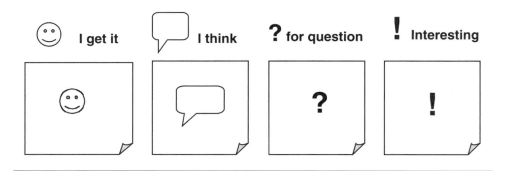

SQ3R Study Strategy

SQ3R stands for Survey, Question, Read, Recite, Review (Anderson & Armbruster, 1984):

- Survey: This step gives the reader a chance to examine the material to check out the headings and have a chance to skim the content. This provides an overview and helps students to access any prior knowledge connected to the reading.
- Question: Students create a question for each section before they read it. The heading may give them a starting point for creating the question. This provides a focus and purpose for the reading that students have created for themselves.
- Read: Each student individually reads the section to answer the question.
- Recite: After the reading students are encouraged to recite the information that they have learned from the passage to answer the question. Students may choose to answer the question orally or in writing.
- Review: After the reading is finished, students review the questions and try to recall the answers to each from memory. If they haven't taken notes previously, now would be the time to write them.

Teachers may provide an SQ3R prompt list (see Figure 5.3) or a note-taking or summarizing organizer to facilitate complete notes.

Reciprocal Teaching

Reciprocal teaching includes a dialogue that takes place between the teacher and students (or student leader) that results in students learning how to construct meaning when they are placed in "must-read" situations, such as tests or assignments. Sometimes it is referred to as "study reading."

Figure 5.3   Prompts for SQ3R study strategy

3	Survey	Look over the assignment
	Question	Make up questions for each heading
	Read	Read the information
	Recite	Tell the answers
	Review	Make notes to answer the questions

The process consists of the four steps of generating questions, summarizing, clarifying, and predicting. This strategy integrates all aspects of literacy: speaking, listening, reading, and writing. It is a great strategy for the English language learner because it facilitates lots of dialogue in a safe and structured environment:

- Generating questions: Students generate questions that they share and answer individually and collectively with supporting material and rationale.
- Summarizing: Students identify key points and develop a summary of the information read.
- Clarifying: Restating or paraphrasing deepens understanding because to restate, one must clearly comprehend the material. At this point new language and terms will need to be clarified.
- Predicting: Students then make assumptions, predictions, and generalizations from the information that has been considered.

During the predicting stage when studying a piece of literature, for example, students may predict what will happen in the next chapter. In social studies, it could be generating a hypothesis for what students think will occur next or implications for the future or based on their new knowledge.

Question Swap

Question Swap (see Figure 5.4) can help focus the learner and create reading with a purpose as well as assist in constructing personal questions about the new information. The directions for Question Swap are as follows:

1. Make up two questions about the given topic.

2. Make sure you know how to answer your own questions.

3. For your first question, find one partner and swap (trade) questions.

4. Then answer your partner's first question and include your name.

5. Repeat steps 3 and 4 with a second partner for your second question.

More Graphic Organizers for Summarizing and Note Taking

Split-page notes (see Table 5.7) help the student actively process information through multiple modes of verbal and written information and

Figure 5.4   Question swap for partner reading

```
┌─────────────────────────────────────────────────────────────┐
│                                                               │
│   Topic_____          Name _____        │
│                                                               │
│                        ┌───┐                                  │
│   QUESTION:           ( ? )                                   │
│                        └───┘                                  │
│                                                               │
│   ANSWER:             💡                                      │
│                                                               │
│                                Name _____         │
│                                                               │
│                                                               │
└─────────────────────────────────────────────────────────────┘
```

```
┌─────────────────────────────────────────────────────────────┐
│                                                               │
│   Topic_____          Name _____        │
│                                                               │
│                        ┌───┐                                  │
│   QUESTION:           ( ? )                                   │
│                        └───┘                                  │
│                                                               │
│   ANSWER:             💡                                      │
│                                                               │
│                                Name _____         │
│                                                               │
│                                                               │
└─────────────────────────────────────────────────────────────┘
```

then organize it into visual forms or graphic organizers. Dual processing engages both hemispheres of the brain and helps in comprehension and long-term memory.

A W5 organizer (see Table 5.8) can be used to take notes while reading a textbook. This organizer works well with social studies content. It also

Table 5.7   Split-page notes to engage both sides of the brain

Jot down key words	Use a graphic organizer

taps into the thinking skills of prediction. This organizer is great for students who are "clipboards" because they love the clear, concrete organization of it. It helps "beach balls" be more organized. If "puppies" get to work with a partner, they would enjoy the activity much more, and the "microscopes" like the opportunity to be analytical or organize as well as compare and contrast.

Cross-classification charts (see Figures 5.5–5.8) help students to organize and record information that can serve as a review and a chance for active processing. These charts also help show relationships and connections. They can be especially useful in organizing thoughts in the prewriting process. We've shown samples for a variety of topics in science—planets (Figure 5.5), flowers and plants (Figure 5.6), and seasons (Figure 5.7)—as well as a reproducible template that teachers can give students for note taking and classifying on other subjects (Figure 5.8).

Also useful for note taking and summarizing while reading a textbook is the four-corner graphic organizer. Figure 5.9 shows how a student might collect details for a science unit about different species. This can be done in a "dot/jot" fashion, where students just record a few words beside a dot or bullet.

Table 5.8   W5 organizer for note taking and summarizing

Topic:	Words	Pictures	What Next?
Who?			
What?			
Where?			
When?			
Why?			
Summary:			

Figure 5.5 Cross-classification chart to use for studying planets

Criteria / Compare these	Size	Distance from Sun	Weather	Surface
Earth				
Mars				
Saturn				
Pluto				

Figure 5.6 Cross-classification chart to use for studying flowers and plants

Criteria / Compare these	Roots	Stem	Leaves	Petals
Rose				
Begonia				
Daffodil				
Petunia				

Figure 5.7 Cross-classification chart to use for studying seasons

Criteria Compare these	Weather	Sports	Clothes	Temperature
Winter				
Spring				
Summer				
Fall				

Figure 5.8 Cross-classification chart for note taking and classifying

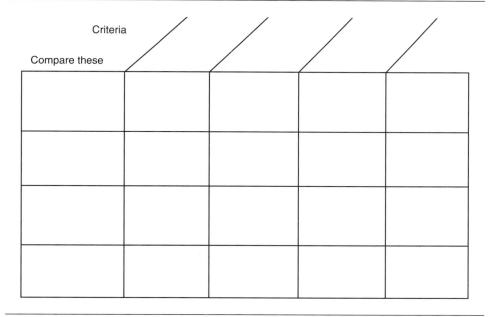

Figure 5.9 Four-corner organizer for studying science

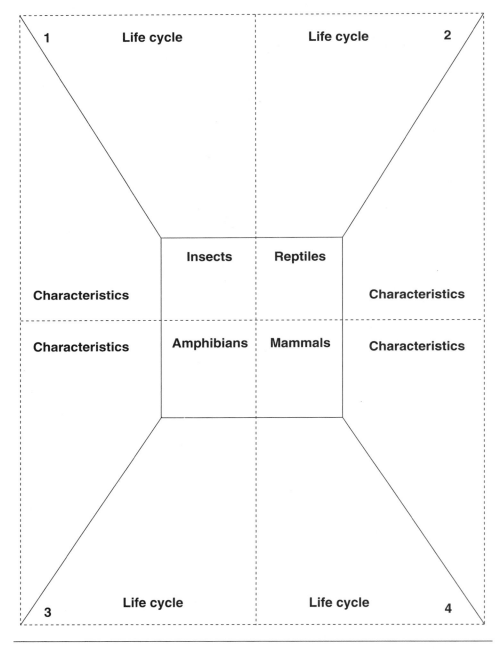

FORMS OF WRITING: EXPOSITORY AND PERSUASIVE

In Chapter 4 on functional literacy, we discussed narrative and descriptive writing. Here we want to discuss expository and persuasive, or influential writing in relation to content learning. Table 5.9 offers basic definitions of expository and persuasive writing.

Table 5.9 Strategies for supporting student growth in expository and persuasive writing

Expository Writing	Persuasive Writing
Purpose: To **provide** information	**Purpose:** To **influence** others
Definitions:	**Definitions:**
• Gives details by using who, what, when, where, and why • Tells step-by-step • Gives directions, or tells how-to • Recollections or reflections	• Makes every effort to convince and change another's mind • Provides an opinion or point of view • Provides evidence to support point of view • May include personal beliefs • Uses persuasive language • Has a target audience • Culminates with a final argument
Have students:	**Have students:**
Write in a journal or diary Write manuals, recipes, and how-to directions Write news stories Retell a story Create factual reports, research papers Perform note taking and summarizing Write book reports	Write a speech to sway an audience Write an editorial to share beliefs Write for brochures to influence others Attempt to convince Create advertisements

Expository Writing

Expository writing is nonfiction. Generally, it uses factual information to recount, inform, or direct the reader. Through expository writing, young children can learn and practice sequence, precision, and accuracy in conveying information to the reader. Expository writing also helps students learn how to read manuals and directions, having had the experience of creating them themselves. Through expository writing, students will learn to do the following:

- Give details by using who, what, when, where, and why
- Tell procedure step by step
- Give directions or tell the how-to
- Recall, reflect, and recount

Table 5.10 offers an organizer that can help students collect data about their recount in a way that flows logically and will enable them to write clearly.

Sometimes teachers begin with simple directions and ask students to work with partners to create a "how-to book" (see Figure 5.10), which might contain directions for the following:

- How to make a bed
- How to wash the dishes
- How to bathe a dog
- How to change the fishbowl water
- How to make scrambled eggs
- How to make a taco
- How to make a smoothie

Students may also be asked to recount an event or experience such as follows:

- Going to the zoo
- Going to the movies
- Going to my friend's home for a sleepover
- Going to a baseball game
- Going to the animal shelter to adopt a dog
- Going to a pioneer village
- Going to visit _____

Explaining how-to and recounting events taps into students' personal experiences in their "real, everyday world," which is one of the richest resources for writing and thinking. It also allows all students, of whatever background or culture, to feel respected in the things they do daily in their lives. These topics are responsive to gender preferences and help English language learners work with the past tense.

Students also may recall and recount a story they have read as a reflection task using an advance organizer to help guide their thinking and planning. Students may want to cover details in chronological order or by following the prompts in the advance organizer templates shown in Figure 5.11 and Table 5.11. If a student is researching factual information in a content area like math, science, social studies, or health, the teacher may want to adjust or replace the prompts on the left-hand side of Table 5.11, depending on what works best with the content being taught.

Table 5.10   Recount organizer for expository writing

Recount

Title: _____

Setting: (Who, What, Where, When, Why):

- _____
- _____
- _____
- _____
- _____

Events:

1. _____

   _____

2. _____

   _____

3. _____

   _____

4. _____

   _____

Closing Statement:

Figure 5.10   How-to organizer for a procedure plan

Topic: _____

Goal:

Equipment:

✓   ✓
✓   ✓
✓   ✓
✓   ✓
✓

Steps:

1.   7.
2.   8.
3.   9.
4.   10.
5.   11.
6.   12.

How did I do?
What was done well?
Was I clear?
Were the steps in a good order?
What did I leave out?
What should I remember next time?
Could someone else follow my directions?

Figure 5.11   Recall/Recount template

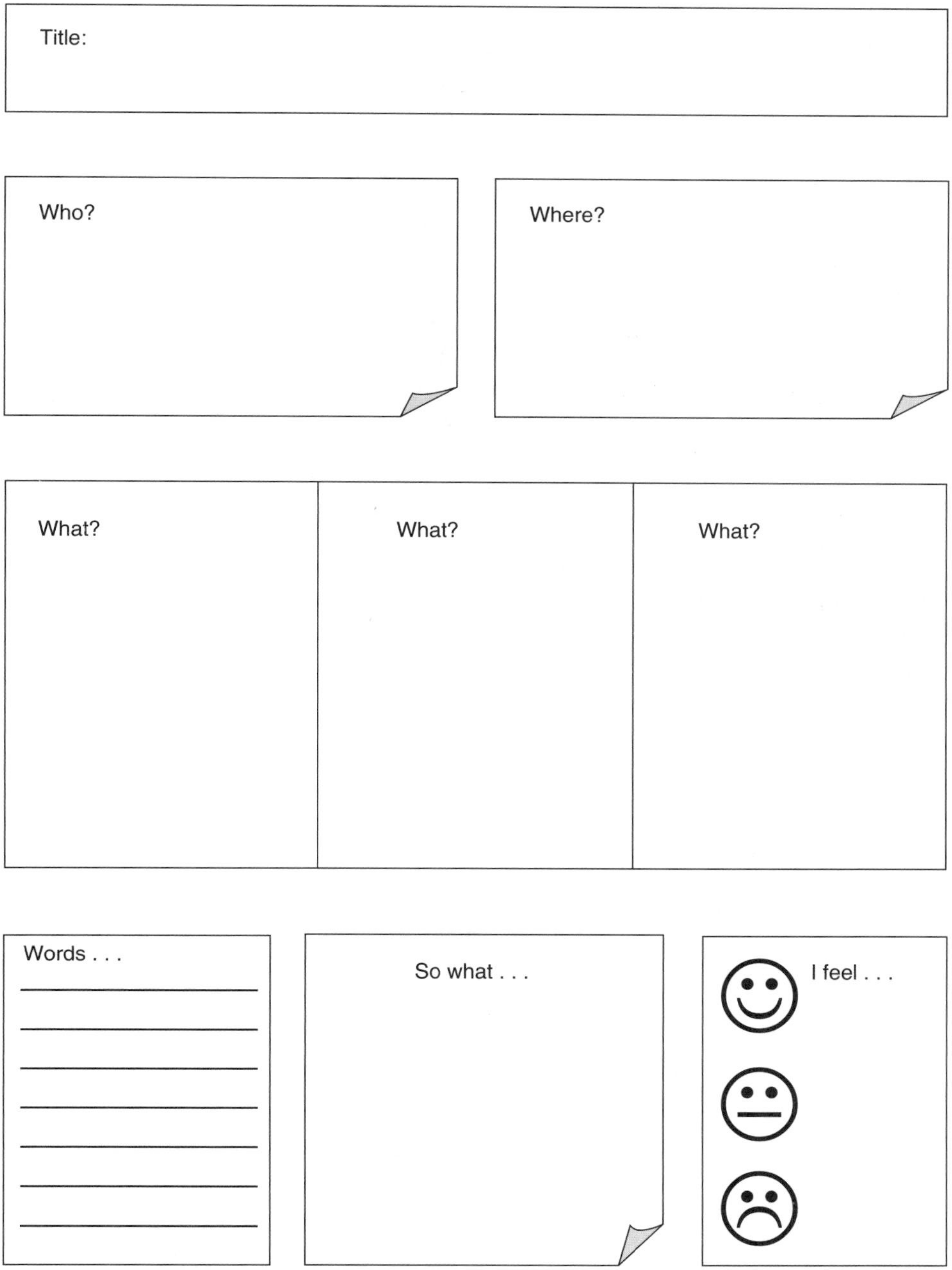

Title:

Who?

Where?

What?

What?

What?

Words . . .

So what . . .

I feel . . .

Table 5.11   Advance organizer for student content report

Preparing My Report	
Title:	Name:
What is it?	
Describe it (size, shape, color):	
Place/Time: Where is it? When is it?	
What does it do?	
Summarizing Comments:	

After writing, students may critically assess their recount using the following checklist:

How Did I Do?

1. I included *Who . . . Where . . . When?* □

2. I explained *What* happened? □

3. I included important events? □

4. My events were in the right order? □

5. I used good linking words (next, after)? □

6. I wrote a good ending sentence? □

7. I did the best job I could do? □

Formulating Questions for Expository Writing

Formulating questions before, during, and after expository writing promotes critical thinking. It helps students to convey meaning, voice, and purpose with greater depth and clarity (Paul & Elder, 2001). Elementary students might use a checklist like the following to prepare for thoughtful writing:

- What is this about?
- Who will read this writing?
- Why should someone read my work?
- What do I want someone to get from my writing?
- Does my writing make sense?
- Do I have details that make my writing easy to understand?
- Do I stay with the idea I started in my writing?
- Are my facts correct?
- Did I use evidence to help readers understand my writing?
- Did I correct all my errors?
- Would I be proud to share my writing?

Organizing Information for Expository Writing

Most textbooks are organized with information in five common patterns. We can facilitate student writing and reading and the organization of information by using graphic organizers that support the five patterns:

1. Description

2. Sequence

3. Cause and effect

4. Compare and contrast

5. Problem and solution

The descriptive web organizer (see Figure 5.12) helps take a concept or topic and organize attributes around the central idea. This helps the student organize information in a visual, logical, and mathematical way. It can also be used to generate descriptive language for writing purposes. Descriptive wheels (see Figure 5.13) extend the web organizer to subcategories that further organize and extend thinking. Students may begin with a central idea such as early explorers and then extend their thinking to the four explorers who were first to discover America.

Sequencing is a thinking skill that helps students with the writing process or to relate a series of events in any subject discipline, such as a process in science or stages in a historical event. It can also be used as a storyboard or in pictorial form to show order in a recount or retell (see Figure 5.14).

Figure 5.12 Descriptive web

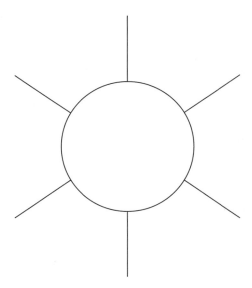

Figure 5.13 Descriptive wheels

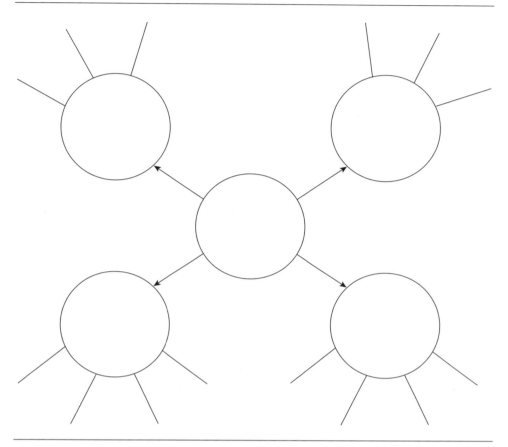

The ability to compare and contrast is a critical thinking skill that is helpful in retaining information through rehearsal and organization of key elements or attributes of two or more items. In Figure 5.15 the two things being compared are placed in the boxes at the top of the page. Then each column of data is organized based on the categories that are placed in the arrow. The similarities of both columns can be placed in the ovals that are labeled "Same." Then the students brainstorm what they know about each topic in each box. After the information has been organized by like or unlike attributes, students should be able to do a quick write to explain the connections.

Figure 5.14   Graphic organizer for sequencing or storyboarding a recount/retell

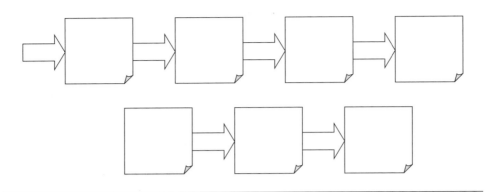

The fish bone organizer (see Figure 5.16) helps examine cause and effect and can also be used for problem solving. The issue or problem to be solved is placed in the front box, and then categories relating to the topic are placed in the horizontal boxes. Attributes are added on the fish bones.

Persuasive Writing

Persuasive writing is expository writing with an influence. In persuasive, or influential, writing, one's purpose is to convince or change another's mind based on evidence, logic, or emotion. It may be based on the writer's opinion as supported by facts, but it usually covers a specific sequence as shown in Table 5.12.

Students may find it interesting to uncover how persuasion is used in everyday life by analyzing television commercials, advertisements, political speeches and posters, movie trailers, newspaper editorials, flyers, and book or movie reviews. Collecting vocabulary of "Words of Influence" has great appeal to students and can be a good bulletin board project.

A great preassessment for persuasive writing is to ask the students to do a quick write to convince the teacher not to give homework the next day. The perceived payoff is clear to the students, and this preassessment quickly lets the teacher know if students have influential words in

Figure 5.15 Compare and contrast flowchart

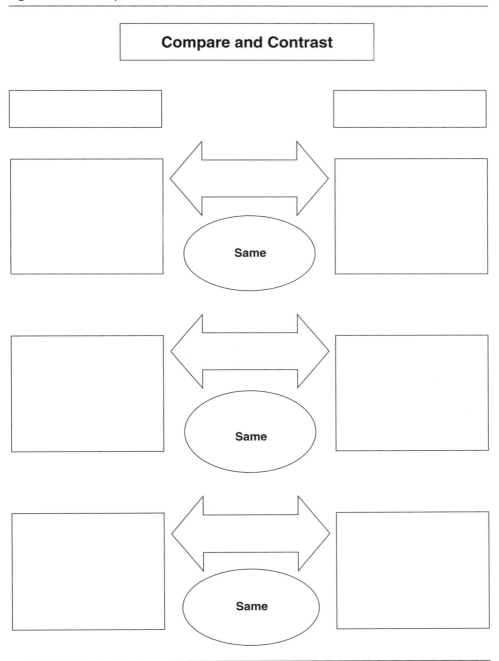

Figure 5.16 Fish bone organizer for attributes or cause and effect

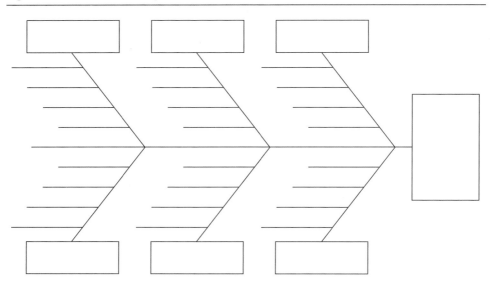

Table 5.12 Sequence for persuasive writing

Opening	Stating the opinion or beliefs
Body	Supporting evidence and facts Developing logical argument Appealing to emotions and feelings Using language of influence
Conclusion	Summarizing Compelling finish

their vocabulary and whether they can formulate an argument in a compelling way.

Book reports can also be a persuasive writing activity, as can letters to a newspaper editor, principal, or local agency that students want to influence. A speech for a class election or about a topic for which a student has a true passion are also ways students may apply and practice their persuasive writing skills. Persuasive writing is also linked to Innovative Literacy, which we will cover in detail in Chapter 7.

PRESENTATION AND PRODUCT CREATION FOR CONTENT AREA LITERACY

Rehearsal of content and elaboration of information can be done in many ways that reinforce literacy skills as well. Students can use their individual learning styles and multiple intelligences to show what they know in positive ways that engage them in learning and create novel experiences.

The choice boards shown in Table 5.13 can be used to review and reinforce content as well as to apply all the kinds of writing, including narrative, descriptive, expository, and persuasive. Choice boards can also be used to align the multiple intelligences with content standards while maintaining a focus on student growth. By helping learners accelerate the acquisition of literacy skills, teachers help them to develop comprehension, rehearse concepts, and refine ideas in all content areas.

Table 5.13   Sample choice boards for young learners

Butterflies

Create a dance showing the life cycle of the butterfly	Pretend that you are a butterfly emerging from a chrysalis. Write about what you will do using the facts you have learned	Make a pattern on the wings of a paper butterfly with tissue paper that is symmetrical
Using a Venn diagram, compare and contrast a butterfly and moth	**Free Choice!**	Write a cinquain pattern poem about a butterfly
Talk about and decide which habitat is best for a butterfly. Show with a diorama or poster	Construct and label the parts of a caterpillar or butterfly	Complete a word find or a crossword puzzle on the life cycle of a butterfly

(Continued)

Table 5.13 (Continued)

Math measurements

Create a song or rap to define measurement concepts (area, volume, perimeter)	Create an acrostic poem using one of the following vocabulary words: perimeter, area, volume, centimeter, or square	Prove it! Volume of the cube 216 cubic inches (cube was 6 inches × 6 inches × 6 inches). Explain how the volume was found
How big is your stride? Count the number of strides it takes to walk the length of the gym. Divide your steps by the actual length of the gym (e.g., 90 feet). How big is each stride?	**Free Choice!**	Measure the sides of a basketball court. Create a scale drawing using the following scale (10 meters = 1 centimeter)
Find the perimeter and the area of the room to the nearest foot and square foot. Pair with partner to check answer. Share with another group of two	Describe situations where you see perimeter, area, or volume being used. Explain why this measurement is used	Watering the lawn! Take a gallon of water. Pour the water into a cup. How many cups equal one gallon?

Chicago

Design a brochure or poster to encourage people to visit Chicago	Create a rap, song, or poem about one of the historical figures of Chicago	Create a skit containing historical facts about Chicago
Write a journal entry about the day of the Chicago fire. Reflect on the events, feelings, and results	**Free Choice!**	Write a biography of a famous Chicagoan. Create questions for an interview with him or her
Name, locate, and compare Lake Michigan with another Great Lake	Create a topographical relief map of Chicago	Draw and explain flora and fauna indigenous to the Chicago area

Days, Weeks, and Months

Sing a "days of the week" song	Illustrate a calendar page for each month showing weather	Survey classmates to find their favorite months and make a bar graph to show the results
Write the days of the week	**Free Choice!**	Match the months of the year using cards in a memory game
Make up a skit with a partner where you show what you do on a weekday and your partner shows what he or she does for a weekend	Demonstrate the number of days in each month using your knuckles	Interview a classmate to learn about a favorite holiday month. Discover why it is his or her favorite

Technological 6
Literacy

TECHNOLOGICAL LITERACY DEFINED

We define technological literacy as using reading, writing, speaking, and listening in multimedia venues to create products and demonstrations of learning. Accessing, using, and creating technology-based tools and strategies promotes multidimensional thinking and production across all the content areas and literacies.

The critical factors in technological literacy include the following:

- Questioning authenticity: applying criteria to establish author and Web site credibility; detecting assumptions, purpose, and clarity
- Searching for information: utilizing the nature and structure of Web-based information to find what you need, demonstrate dimensional or embedded thinking, and solve problems
- Media orientation: what is the best method for the product and meaning you must convey or produce
- Production: utilizing computer-based and other multimedia production to demonstrate literacy competencies and produce products to convey meaning, solutions, and adaptations
- Demystifying directions: understanding and using directions in multiple forms and verbal or written construction of sequential steps for use of technological and other tools and processes

THE MULTIDIMENSIONAL NATURE OF THE TWENTY-FIRST CENTURY

Technological literacy starts with some basic understandings that have transformed our process for acquisition, comprehension, and use of information.

Most of us learned to teach in a linear fashion up until very recently, but the twenty-first century is primarily about multidimensional thinking. Think about what it was like to go from using a print version of an encyclopedia to doing Internet-based research instead. That is the essence of multidimensional thinking. Looking up a key word or topic in a book is a very different literacy skill from conducting an effective Internet search using search engines and logic to refine a search strategy.

Looking something up in a book requires us to hold certain information in our brains as we conduct our search. During an Internet search, we use dimensional and spatial aspects of thought, holding information in an almost three-dimensional array as we move through the refinement of a topic and search patterns. And when we visit each identified Web site, we must still decide if the site has value by applying criteria we have learned or developed.

The American Library Association describes six stages of a process that takes place continuously in true technological literacy (Ryan & Capra, 2001):

1. Defining

2. Locating

3. Selecting and analyzing

4. Organizing and synthesizing

5. Creating and presenting

6. Evaluating

These steps are not linear. They involve spatial multitasking, and they must be synchronized (see Table 6.1).

QUESTIONING AUTHENTICITY

Anyone can develop a Web site with the right technological skills, and many with those same skills can publish. So how do we teach young children to understand the relative value of information sources?

Table 6.1   Technological and information literacy

Stage	Student Actions for Literacy
1. Defining	<ul><li>Formulates questions that clarify</li><li>Refines problem or task through questions</li><li>Identifies key words</li><li>Predicts results</li><li>Formulates hypothesis-like questions as refinement progresses</li><li>Uses modeled techniques</li><li>Self-evaluates clarity of questions</li><li>Establishes increasing focus</li><li>Further refines questions at each click until the problem or task reaches a level of usable definition for the search</li></ul>
2. Locating	<ul><li>Follows a search plan</li><li>Recognizes currency of information</li><li>Looks for multiple viewpoints</li><li>Uses primary and secondary sources</li><li>Recognizes purpose and intent</li><li>Generates examples to deepen understanding</li><li>Understands the strengths and weaknesses of search engines</li><li>Accesses government and research-based sources</li></ul>
3. Selecting and Analyzing	<ul><li>Skims and scans</li><li>Keeps a multidimensional view of a visited sites in mind to effectively navigate (thinks in site map terms)</li><li>Clusters and combines information</li><li>Develops a method of recording and saving needed information or sites</li><li>Uses accepted Web site visual clues to find information (tabs, buttons, boxes, color, print size and boldness, site maps, etc.)</li><li>Compares and contrasts information from multiple sites and resources</li><li>Collects an adequate body of evidence or information before drawing a conclusion</li><li>Complies with electronic copyright laws</li><li>Devises electronic note taking methods that suit personal preferences</li><li>Records bibliographic information</li><li>Looks actively for bias, omissions, and errors</li><li>Spots contradictions</li><li>Recognizes positive and negative influences</li></ul>
4. Organizing and Synthesizing	<ul><li>Develops categories for located information</li><li>Constructs generalizations using evidence and draws logical conclusions</li><li>Uses headings and print formatting to emphasize a point</li><li>Creates graphical representations and inserts appropriately</li><li>Recognizes deficiencies in information through self-evaluation questioning</li></ul>

(Continued)

Table 6.1 (Continued)

Stage	Student Actions for Literacy
4. Organizing and Synthesizing	• Shows sophisticated synthesis of information from a variety of sources • Creates alternative solutions • Clearly states and understands consequences of conclusions • Consolidates information • Creates models and examples to make a point • Makes appropriate inferences from nondirectly stated information • Connects ideas • Applies ethical principles to use of information as well as conclusions • Verifies conclusions • Suggests future refinements or ideas for improvement
5. Creating and Presenting	• Identifies audience and purpose • Selects media that suits required reporting elements • Demonstrates creative use of multiple elements • Uses a constructivist approach as needed • Logical presentation of ideas • Provides sufficient material given problem or task • Understands and utilizes formatting elements and media to advantage • Work is persuasive and compelling • Vocabulary is specific to task
6. Evaluating	• Self-evaluates work given criteria or creates appropriate criteria from a variety of sources • Accepts feedback from peers or others and makes appropriate changes in presentation • Evaluates audience understanding and appreciation of presentation • Uses models effectively to improve and create presentations • Analyzes accuracy of problem and solution given resources and criteria • Sets goal for present project and for future projects • Shows effective analysis of problem-solving strategies applied to the project

Source: For a fuller discussion of this topic, see Ryan and Capra (2001).

Most youngsters understand truth and lying as a linear feature of the same piece of information. Understanding that the truth can be viewed in many ways depending on the truth-teller's purpose and perspective is much harder to teach during the earlier stages of child development. At the elementary level, however, students *can* be empowered with questions that help them do three things (see Table 6.2):

Table 6.2   Questioning authenticity

Questioning for Clarity	Questioning Assumptions	Questioning to Detect Bias
Is the information clear?	What is the point of view of the author or creator?	What is the date of the information?
Are there examples that make sense?	What is the author's purpose for presenting this information? How do you know?	Can you easily find other sources that say the same thing?
Is it easy to restate in your own words?	What question does this information answer?	Does the author use too many emotion words? Is this opinion or fact?
Can you find enough details?	What conclusions does the author draw? Are they logical?	Is there contact information such as an e-mail address? Where does the author work?

Source: Adapted from the work of Paul and Elder (2002).

- Seek clarity
- Question assumptions
- Detect source reliability or bias

Younger elementary students, however, will need the information they use preselected by the teacher, but that gives the teacher an excellent opportunity to tell students why he or she picked a particular site or source and to model the strategies that students will need to use independently in the near future. Another way to reaffirm these concepts is to have students do a "quick write" about a site or source of information after they use it. Figure 6.1 offers prompts that can be used with younger students. The American Library Association (http://www.ala.org) is an excellent source of age-appropriate templates, toolkits, and organizers that can help students learn about questioning authenticity of research materials.

SEARCHING FOR INFORMATION

Information searches require the multidimensional thinking we discussed above. We can begin to represent such thinking in terms of flowcharts or organizers that have levels of understanding or complexity of concepts.

Figure 6.1   Prompts for a quick write about an information source or Web site

In one sentence, tell why this source was helpful:	List three things you like about this site:

Share with the author: 1. What was good about the information? 2. What should the author change?	List three things that make this information easy to use:

Search Engines

When we used periodical guides or lists of books in print in the library to search for information, our tools were scraps of paper with titles on them and, later, photocopies. With a clear purpose in mind, we looked in the guides for sources of information and then physically located the relevant book or journal on the library shelves, but Internet searches are different. We select various kinds of search engines to begin the search, we choose key words, and then we use special languages (i.e., Boolean logic) to refine our search strategies.

With young children in second and third grade, we can specify and teach them how to use search engines that are specially designed for such purposes. It is helpful for students to map out their searches to help them get used to thinking in terms of gradual refinement of topics (see Figure 6.2).

The boxes in our topic organizer model get bigger when our students acquire more specific and useful information as they refine their searches. Good searches start with a good question or a good premise. As students learn to refine their questions (see Figure 6.3), they get better search results.

Figure 6.2   Learning to refine topics in a search for information

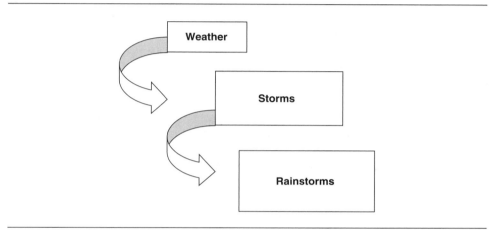

Figure 6.3   Learning to refine questions in a search for information

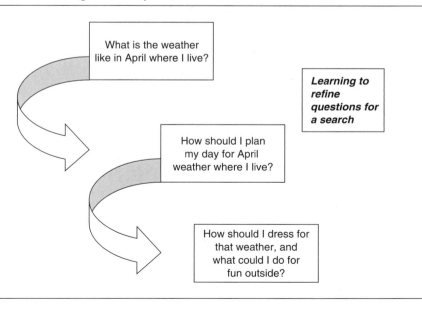

Setting Search Goals

Another important concept in searches for information is the idea of matching the information to the purpose or intent behind the questions. That means getting students to ask, why is this information important? and, does it really answer the question?

The underlying structure of the Internet causes information flooding in ways that were not possible with print alone. If students copy down, download, or reword this flood of factual bits and pieces without a clear filtering system in mind, the results will be learning products that lack clarity and depth. Table 6.3 offers an organizer that may help elementary students sort through the mass of information and resources. Teachers can provide a choice in the last box of this planner, or students can create a list of three top choices and then pick the one that best fits their search results or the requirements of the unit assessment.

A simple or detailed planning guide provides a tool for students to navigate the multidimensional nature of searches in an electronic world. As soon as students learn these guided techniques, they can create their own guides or note taking tools to match the goals of their searches or their learning styles. Such planners may include the following:

- Paper and pencil
- Folders with organized sticky notes
- Colorful mind maps
- Colored paper shapes to indicate levels of search or questions
- Electronic graphics creators, such as Inspiration Software
- Electronic embedded screens with buttons or arrows
- A large story board
- Other methods that suit the student's learning style and the desired project results

Students who use a rubric (or, for younger learners, a checklist) may find building a planning tool to be an easier task. In that case, they may be able to help other learners who lack organization by encouraging them to be creative or by sharing prompts and templates to help them initiate or complete the tasks.

MEDIA ORIENTATION

Students need to select a method of demonstrating and communicating what they have learned that:

- Matches the unit assessment
- Answers the key questions

Table 6.3   Search planning with a goal in mind (for third grade and up)

Name:	Class:	Date:
My big question:	A smaller question about part of my big question:	A smaller question about part of my big question:
Search engine choice:	Three words to start my search that come from my big question: 1. 2. 3.	Words to answer my smaller questions: 4. 5. 6. 7.
How will I record information that answers my smaller questions: ❑ Use a web ❑ Use a note taking chart ❑ Draw pictures ❑ List phrases ❑ Use an electronic folder ❑ Another way that works for me:	How I know this information is good or accurate: ❑ Current ❑ Author's background ❑ Other sources say the same thing ❑ Words that tell about information and where they got it	Why is this information important to answer my smaller questions: ❑ Gives me facts ❑ Helps me understand ❑ Shows me how ❑ Answers part of my question ❑ Other:_____ _____
How will I record information that answers my big question: ❑ Use a web ❑ Use a note taking chart ❑ Draw pictures ❑ List phrases ❑ Use an electronic folder ❑ Another way that works for me:	How I know this information is good or accurate: ❑ Current ❑ Author's background ❑ Other sources say the same thing ❑ Words that tell about information and where they got it	Why is this information important to answer my big question: ❑ Gives me facts ❑ Helps me understand ❑ Shows me how ❑ Answers part of my question ❑ Other:_____ _____
What is a project or way I can tell others about what I discovered and how I will use the information? (Fill this out before your search, then make any changes after your search.)		

- Uses variety appropriate for the topic
- Fits the purpose for the project or product

Figure 6.4 is a planner that can help students select their medium of communication. The planner starts with each block at the same size, but as the student works through the following requirements, certain desired results will cause one block to become larger or more important:

- **Audience:** Students or teachers may choose a different production method or communication method if the audience changes from peers to parents or community members. Some type of performance or demonstration may be more appropriate for parents than just a written report.

- **Rubric or scoring guide:** If the rubric requires a research paper format, that helps limit the options quite a bit. If the rubric describes the written presentation of research and conclusion, students have more production options. Maybe a Microsoft PowerPoint presentation or a set of drawings with brief written information would be acceptable.

- **Questions:** A question about art may need to have art or artistic interpretations in the product. A question about a process may need a demonstration. A question about a system or model may need a model or three-dimensional representations. Without a clear verb in the question, students may have to choose based on the topic. Cultural influences are hard to represent in words alone. Famous people are better described with actions, models, or pictures in addition to words and reports.

- **Purpose:** Informing lends itself to reports that are both oral and written. Persuading lends itself to evidence prepared through Microsoft PowerPoint or cause and effect models as well as writing. Discovery has all sorts of possibilities, even video or other media.

While there are no hard and fast rules, helping students draw logical conclusions about methods of presentation is an important technological literacy skill for the twenty-first century. Teaching students to think critically in this manner is fun and can be used to help with logical conclusions in tougher situations, like social conflict and ethical sales presentations. Students who discuss the reasons for their choices and have the ability to refine them based on further research and exploration can expand their comprehension.

Reminding students that they are attempting to convey meaning and not just information is helpful. A list of facts is as boring to others as it is to them. Our multimedia culture of television, Internet, and electronic games and environments tells us about how people like to get and use information for a variety of purposes. Knowing these skills not only engages an audience but can expand the learner's eventual scope for work

Figure 6.4   Choosing the right medium for communicating information

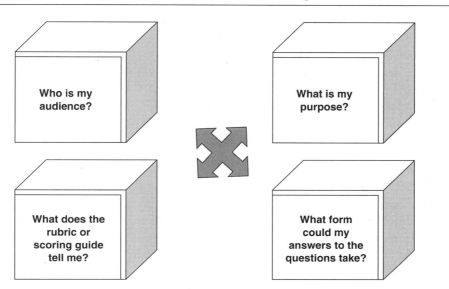

and job skills. Further, matching logical purpose and product are life skills. This kind of technological literacy has great potential for English language learners, who can use the Internet to acquire their new language rapidly, find visual representations, and learn hidden meanings of words and dialogue in a media-rich environment.

MULTIMEDIA PRODUCTION

Multimedia production lends itself well to apprenticeship thinking. Students need models, a friendly mentor or guide, written direction, criteria for levels of quality, and opportunities for rehearsal and practice.

Production is more than knowing how to create a Microsoft PowerPoint presentation. It is also about conveying meaning and purpose. Do you remember grainy black and white or brown and off-white photography? Comparing earlier photos to digital photography now is clear evidence that quality indicators change over time as more and newer media options become available over time. Technological literacy is about using information and media to adapt to change. This is certainly a lifelong learner skill for the twenty-first century.

Teacher Comfort and Proficiency

Production opportunities are not often limited in classrooms by student abilities but by the comfort levels of their teachers. Many schools and districts now require staff to learn technology basics as a job requirement. This expectation for application and opportunities is not only appropriate but also necessary in a world of diversity and change. Teachers who know how to use, or allow their students to use, a variety of multimedia options to convey meaning and understanding will have better results than teachers who use a limited array of choices.

Multidimensional and multimedia opportunities help students expand their thinking skills as they use literacy skills. The modified graphic organizer shown in Figure 6.5 can help with that task, especially if it is used in an electronic format. By transferring the organizer to an online format, the resulting product becomes more fluid and can change more easily as new knowledge is added. Such habits of modification and adjustment also add to the thinking skills and behaviors that students need as they adapt to constant change and complex real-life problems. There are many types of software that support this kind of template creation, some with additional buttons, media, or embedded features. Some top-notch favorites of ours include Inspiration Software, Microsoft PowerPoint or Publisher, Adobe Products, HyperStudio, Kid Pix, and many others. Just look for the capabilities we have described.

Figure 6.5   A graphic organizer template for searches using modified semantic feature analysis (Grades 4–6)

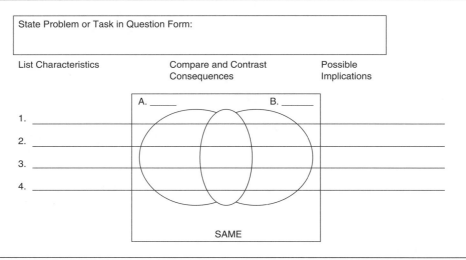

Production Elements

1. **Solution orientation:** Production that supports solution finding and creation is also a key characteristic of technological literacy. Appropriately evaluating the quality of the production is an important factor.

2. **Preplanning:** Story mapping a video on an electronic board is a part of production and may be a criterion on a quality indicator checklist or rubric.

3. **Appropriate and relevant:** Logical connection to the purpose, audience, assessment, and key questions.

4. **Evaluation:** Peer evaluation and self-evaluation are important elements in production using technological literacy. A checklist of criteria should be available before a project begins (see Figure 6.6). Models or exemplars from previous student work are also essential to help students develop appropriate self- and peer-evaluation skills.

5. **Demonstrates literacy competencies:** This includes searching for and using information from a variety of sources; conveying meaning; and selecting, sorting, and prioritizing data for solution development.

Sample Technological Self-Evaluation Questions

- Do my pictures tell about the problem?
- Does the video clip show enough evidence to support my conclusion?
- Is my electronic slide show organized?
- Can my audience understand my final product? Are the words easy to read and the pictures easy to see?
- Did I explain how I got my answer?
- Did I demonstrate the steps in the right order?
- How well does my oral presentation match the electronic demonstration or visual aids?

DEMYSTIFYING DIRECTIONS

Technological literacy is also about understanding and following directions. Not many of us use software manuals, most of which are now electronic, except to look up specific information or to get answers

Figure 6.6   Organizer for a technology presentation

My Technology Presentation Plan

Question this presentation answers:

Sources:

Time it will take to deliver:

Audio Plan:	**Video Plan:**
Δ Voice (oral report)	Δ Shots
Δ Music	Δ Clips
Δ Dialogue	Δ Sequence
Δ Sequence	Δ Dialogue or sounds
Δ Sound clips	Δ Graphics or labels
Δ Other _____	Δ Other _____
Print Plan:	**Technology-Assisted Demonstration Plan:**
Δ Software	Δ A computerized play or action game
Δ Format	Δ Computer generated simulation or how-to demo
Δ Text type	
Δ Graphics	Δ International debate with pen pal
Δ Clips	Δ Electronically created song
Δ Sequence	Δ Computer-based experiment
Δ Other _____	Δ Other _____

Figure 6.7 Direction words for technological literacy

<table>
<tr>
<td>

Familiar Direction Words:

- Organize
- Synthesize
- Infer hidden meanings
- Sequence words
- Analyze
- Compare
- Edit
- Clarify
- Categorize
- Causes
- Find or locate
- Retell
- Discuss
- Steps

</td>
<td>

Technology-Based Direction Words:

- Boolean logic
- Browse
- Download
- Program
- Search engine use
- Merge
- Format
- Auto-summarize
- Slide
- Convert
- Customize
- Preference settings
- Wrap text

</td>
</tr>
</table>

to questions. Jokes about people who cannot program DVD players or VCR clocks are widespread and well-known, but giving others direction and following directions are important life skills. Literacy in technology means doing both along with the ability to produce or find something as a result of following directions.

Technological literacy, understanding directions in particular, require us to use some familiar words and concepts, but many technological words and concepts are new (see Figure 6.7).

We can teach our students direction words that are familiar, but how much time do we spend with technological words and directions? In fact, teachers may not give students enough rehearsal in this area because our students often are more familiar with the meanings of these words than we are. Using students as tutors and peer coaches for technological literacy can work well in offering practice opportunities and rehearsal.

Using analogies and examples that contain technological language found in directions helps students begin to use this vocabulary in writing, product creation, evaluation, and oral presentations. Clarity with directions and practice also helps students with learning styles and multiple intelligences with more linguistic orientation. This is where our spatial, visual, and kinesthetic learners can help others.

TECHNOLOGICAL LITERACY AND DIVERSE LEARNERS

The Gender Gap and the Spatial Learning Factor

One of the reasons boys score better than girls on math tests has to do with boys' ability to use "fast spatial" reasoning while girls use slower "linguistic" methods (Thornberg, 1991): "This work strongly suggests that we need to develop the spatial reasoning ability of all children—especially girls"(Thornberg, 1991, p. 5).

When time is a factor, the gender differences become evident, showing up in high-stakes assessments in math, which use time as a factor. When time is not a factor, boys and girls score more equally. Technology literacy requires an increased spatial sense from all learners. Spatial sense development can be cultivated through many media, including the following:

- Graphics
- Music creation
- Games
- Graphic organizer programs
- Computerized map creation
- Hypermedia presentations

Most forms of embedded and space-related functions that require geometric insights can assist learners in developing spatial reasoning (Thornberg, 1991).

Students With Learning Disabilities and the Spelling Factor

Capitalizing on brain research and the increase in tactile learners reported in recent research, we know that many learners with disabilities need both visual and tactile connections to literacy (Sousa, 2003). Frequently, learners with linguistic or perceptual difficulties in reading and writing have numerous problems in acquiring proficient and fluent spelling or even in recognizing spelling errors. There is reasonable anecdotal research both in technological literacy and in occupational therapy literature to indicate that typing and a "type to learn" process can benefit certain types of students with spelling difficulties (Watts-Taffe, Gwinn, Johnson, & Horn, 2003). The use of color-coded type fonts has been shown to help students develop long-term memories for spelling better than more traditional methods (Andres & Lupart, 1993), and it's likely that all learners (not just those with learning disabilities) may benefit from these strategies.

Ethnic Diversity and the Appropriate Materials Factor

Technology provides us with access to newer teaching materials and resources that do a better job of reflecting diversity than some of our more dated textbooks. Even today, the multicultural content of most textbooks still sits in sidebars and special sections, especially when schools cannot afford newer materials (Loewen, 1995).

Technology and the Internet allow us to demonstrate and honor diversity in our classrooms cost effectively and more frequently than ever before. When John Dewey (1956) wrote about the four primary interests of learners, he cited:

- Inquiry
- Communication
- Construction
- Expression

Those four elements continue to be essential to meeting the needs of diverse learners, especially using technological and multimedia venues for learning (Bruce & Bishop, 2002).

Using technology we can take international tours, course through history, understand cultural and racial contributions, and see a much more colorful world than exists in our older classroom materials. This accessibility is a wonderful way to update our teaching and learning materials and to expose all of our students to the differences that more accurately reflect our society: "It's not just an add-on or an afterthought. Curriculums infused with multicultural education boost academic success and prepare students for roles as productive citizens" (Gay, 2004, p. 30).

True connections with our diversity should be infused on a daily basis, not just in celebration of a holiday or a unit on a single leader or historical event. Students from different groups are going to be more motivated by current and diverse materials, and those are now abundantly accessible.

Using the Internet for current materials is only one aspect. Music, art, and other cultural hallmarks are available on Web sites, but the creation of those elements is also a part of learning, and using computer-assisted methods is another excellent strategy for meeting diverse needs. Communicating and holding virtual conferences with folks from around the world can enrich all forms of literacy acquisition.

TECHNOLOGICAL LITERACY AND LIFELONG LEARNING

We could certainly cite the benefits of technological literacy for each student subgroup or population and find confirming data. However, the key is to teach the technological thinking and literacy skills as well-integrated parts of any reading, writing, speaking, and listening program across grades and content areas.

Students who do not have this access and exposure to technological literacy in our schools will not achieve the necessary level of literacy to function in our technological era. Without the integration of technology skills and applications, students may be disadvantaged more by the instruction they are *not receiving* than by any racial, gender, language, or disability factor: "When we rely on a single source of material for all of a course's content, we are teaching students to accept one view and one authority" (Daniels & Zemelman, 2004, p. 39). That does not prepare us for the twenty-first century. Technological literacy prepares us for the twenty-first century by helping us all become more knowledgeable and adaptive lifelong learners.

Innovative Literacy 7

INNOVATIVE LITERACY DEFINED

We define innovative literacy as reading, writing, speaking, and listening to do a complex task, solve a complex problem, invent a unique product or process, or create something new or influential. Innovative literacy helps learners develop adaptability and a practical orientation to their work and their lives both inside and outside the classroom and school setting. This is the kind of literacy that will help them go beyond survival. This is the key to their thriving amid the rapid change and expansion of knowledge in the twenty-first century.

The critical factors in innovative literacy include the following:

- Innovation and creativity: an entrepreneurial sense of thinking and acting; fluidity and flexibility in the use of information; and the transformation of knowledge into new things, attitudes, solutions, products, or actions
- Lifelong learner orientation: acquiring marketable skills over time; responding to anticipated needs; and creating ways to assimilate and accommodate change, regardless of its pace
- Practical and adaptive thinking: scenario-based thinking and responses to real-life situations; inquiry into and interpretation of new information; consumer skills that are self-selected based on available resources and desired results; and adapting information or interactions to plan and make decisions both for the present and the future
- Innovative and influential communication: going beyond narrative, descriptive, expository, and persuasive writing to communicate new, convincing, and believable points of view; applying rational, ethical, and congruent logic to support positive and creative conclusions and solutions

INNOVATION AND CREATIVITY

What We Know About Innovation

Twenty years from now, when your students are sitting in a meeting, virtual or otherwise, will they be able to generate solutions for whatever problem is under discussion? The answer depends on an often-neglected aspect of literacy: the need to be innovative based on interpretation of information from a variety of sources.

Synonyms for *innovative* and *innovation* include:

• Resourceful	• Improving
• Clever	• Unique
• Inspiring	• Novel
• Visionary	• Inventive
• Creative	• Imaginative
• Advancing	• Fresh
• Original	• Initiative
• Modernizing	• Ingenious

In "real life," innovation also means creating solutions, processes, and products that require skills students need to have learned as part of functional, content area, and technological literacies. Stretching the family budget, relocating for work or retirement, managing both crisis and leisure, and making decisions and understanding consequences are all examples of adults using the innovative literacy skills that they began learning in elementary school.

Innovative Skills

Innovative skills start with a student's ability to gather information and ideas from multiple sources, retrieve prior knowledge and experiences, ask questions, and then assimilate the data and develop solutions, options, processes, products, and other creative possibilities to serve a specific purpose or reach a desired goal. Innovative skills allow students to seek and arrive at answers to the "what if . . ."questions they will encounter in school and in life (Manzo, Barnhill, Land, Manzo, & Thomas, 1997).

This kind of information use and solution seeking are part of the constructive process at the foundation of adult literacy, as confirmed by research on the characteristics of proficient adult readers and communicators: "The seeming more optimized and literate individuals seem to be empathetic, socially sensitive, confident, independent thinking, logical, creative men and women who actively embrace available knowledge and then seek to create and construct new knowledge" (Manzo, Manzo, Barnhill, & Thomas, 2000).

Questioning and Critical Thinking

As with content area literacy and technological literacy, innovation and creativity start with questions. As educators, many of us have had training in forming higher-level questions to enhance the critical thinking of our students. Teaching students to formulate questions has a high payoff. When students do the work of formulating questions, they develop a natural inquisitiveness that has lifelong implications for success (Barell, 2003).

Increasing fluid and flexible questioning in students also increases the quality of the answers our students produce: "The quality of our thinking is given in the quality of our questions. . . . It is not possible to be a good thinker and a poor questioner" (Paul & Elder, 2002, pp. 2–3). Paul and Elder (2002), the U.S. Department of Labor (1991), Barell (2003), Manzo (2003), Sternberg (1996), and other sources suggest several types of questions that help us teach students to become better questioners on their way to achieving innovative and creative literacy (see Table 7.1).

Table 7.1   Student question formation to promote innovation and creativity

Type of Questions That Lead to Innovative Literacy	Descriptions and Purposes for Questions	Examples of Questions
Analytic Questions (Paul & Elder, 2002; U.S. Department of Labor, 1991; Sternberg, 1996; Harvey & Goudvis, 1998)	• Determining purpose • Gathering detailed information • Detecting underlying assumptions • Establishing point of view • Drawing inferences • Comparing and contrasting abstract concepts • Making judgments, evaluations	• What is the purpose of . . .? • Why is that so? • How did you get that answer? • What is the source or reason for . . .?

(Continued)

Table 7.1 (Continued)

Decision Making and Problem Solving Questions (Paul & Elder, 2002; Barell, 2003; Manzo, 2003)	• Choosing between alternatives • Determining the pros and cons • Clarifying and forming a hypothesis, problem statement, or a decision to be made • Establishing parts-to-whole relationships in pertinent information • Articulating needs • Determining strategic (worth and merit) and tactical (method and resources) advantages to solutions • Establishing parameters	• What if . . .? • What will happen if I make this choice? • What is one part of the problem? • Why would I . . .?
Systems Questions (U.S. Department of Labor, 1991; Clements, Kolbe, & Villapando, 2000; Paul & Elder, 2002)	• Understanding social, governmental, and other human interaction systems • Predicting impact on a system or the system's impact on the individual • Diagnosing the need for corrections or changes in actions, behaviors, and performance • Determining ethical and moral orientation • Detecting bias • Determining the status of something in progress • Questioning authenticity	• Where did that information come from? • What will this mean if it happens next time? • Do I need to do something different? • How did you arrive at that opinion? • Will this hurt someone else? • Is this right or wrong? How do I know?
Creativity Questions (Torrance, 1998; Gross, 1990; Sternberg, 1996; Barell, 2003)	• Generating ideas • Creating improvements • Designing new solutions • Building or expanding on other ideas • Creating products or performances • Inquiry or curiosity questions • Enabling imagination • Troubleshooting • Effectively using interrelationships • Questioning the status quo or current thinking	• How can this be improved? • What would make this work or work better? • I wonder what would happen if . . .? • What else could we use this for? • Are there any other good ideas? • What if I drew a picture? • What might be missing?

Curiosity and Healthy Skepticism

Curiosity is a fundamental requirement in innovative literacy. Curiosity is not limited by gender, race, disability, or other differences among us. Pat Wolfe and Ron Brandt (1998) tell us:

> [T]he brain is essentially curious and it must be to survive. It constantly seeks connections between the new and the known. Learning is a process of active construction by the learner. (p. 11)

Our best inventors throughout history have displayed a natural skepticism and ability to question conventional interpretations of systems, products, and behaviors. As teachers, we need to encourage our diverse learners to exercise respectful skepticism on their way to innovation and creativity without seeing skepticism as something to defend or punish. Students who live, think, and learn differently from their teachers sometimes are held to standards that do not allow for healthy inquiry and questioning of the status quo (Payne, 2001). As educators we can ask ourselves whose status quo are we defending and from what prospective? Teaching our students the internal and external dialogue required to be innovative and creative sometimes requires us to confront our own assumptions and points of view.

Intelligence

Sternberg (1996) has identified the three intelligences of learners to address the full range of intelligent behaviors and attitudes students need for success: memory-analytical, creative, and practical abilities. This view of intelligence and the skills needed to demonstrate successful learning represent a more inclusive approach to student growth than measurement by conventional intelligence tests. The type of thinking Sternberg describes is essential in innovative and creative literacy. The interaction of all three types of abilities helps students prepare for and act for the future. Instruction and curriculum that support the development of these essential intelligences are what students need as we prepare them to manage the pace of change in the twenty-first century.

INSTRUCTIONAL STRATEGIES THAT PROMOTE INNOVATIVE AND CREATIVE LITERACY

Here are three strategies that we think have excellent possibilities for diverse students. Four Squares for Creativity (see Table 7.2) is an excellent data collection tool in addition to promoting creative thought. R.A.F.T. (see Table 7.3) and Choice Boards (see Table 7.4) are well-proven strategies that help students develop the fluid and flexible thought patterns essential to innovative thinking, reasoning, elaboration, generalization, and creativity.

Four Squares for Creativity

To use Four Squares for Creativity, the teacher first poses a question or states an issue. In groups, the students then complete the chart shown in Table 7.2 over the course of the middle of the unit to significantly deepen their thinking. When students get good at this, many can create their own Four Squares. This works as well in history and science as it does in art or computer technology (Gregory & Kuzmich, 2004).

The Four Squares method can be used as both an instructional and assessment strategy to promote elaboration and generalization of learning (Paul & Elder, 2002; Marzano, Norford, Paynter, Gaddy, & Pickering, 2001). Appropriate assignments could include the following:

- Examining a topic deeper with a challenging question
- Questioning an expert
- Testing ideas against a model
- Developing criteria for evaluation
- Applying new learning to other situations
- Finding evidence to support or refute a claim
- Developing a new use for something familiar

R.A.F.T.: Role, Audience, Format, Topic

R.A.F.T. is a strategy developed by Buehl (2001) and others that motivates and encourages creative writing and divergent thinking in students. It works this way:

1. Select content from any subject area that students need to process, review, and understand.

2. Consider the possible roles that students might take on in writing about the topic as well as what the topic might be.

3. Offer students the opportunity to assume one of the roles and write the assignment on the topic suggested. Students may also be allowed to create their own R.A.F.T. scenarios.

Choice Boards

As mentioned in Chapter 3, the teacher's ability to understand student learning styles and multiple intelligences is a key factor in differentiating instruction for diverse learners. Choice boards lend themselves to innovative thinking in literacy by promoting flexibility, adaptive thinking, and creativity for individual learners.

Table 7.2   Four squares for creativity

Elementary Example: What kind of tool is best?

List as many uses for a tool as you can in five minutes. Use brainstorming rules. Tool _____ *Fluency*	What kind of tools do you think your parents would like as a gift? You can guess. *Flexibility*
Originality Think of a new tool that everyone needs. Name your tool _____ What will it help us do? _____ _____ Draw your tool	*Elaboration* Describe your tool so that we could use the description in an advertisement on the Internet or in the newspaper.

Table 7.3   R.A.F.T.

Role	Audience	Format	Topic
Buffalo	People	Plea	Prevent extinction
Respiratory System	Smoker	Media advertisement	Infuence to quit smoking
Flower	Earth	Thank-you note	Role in flower's growth
Father	National Rifle Association	Rationale	Gun control
George Bush	Steinbeck	Letter	Reactions to *Of Mice and Men*
Wilbur	Charlotte	Testimonial	Appreciation for saving his life
Salmon	Self	Diary entry	Effects of pollution
Magazine	Readers	Editorial	Importance of eggs

Table 7.4   Choice board for creativity

Interview a character of your choice from the story.	Write a theme song or ballad for the book.	Where are your characters now? Write the sequel.
Write a book review or trailer of a movie.	**Free Choice!**	Create a time line to chronicle the important events of the story.
Act out a favorite part of the book.	Research the author and prepare a report or presentation.	Make a movie poster casting current stars as the lead characters.

Differentiating for Diverse Learners

Many learners are visual or kinesthetic (Sousa, 2003), especially students with disabilities. English Language Learners may need strong initial visual clues, as may some cultural groups; many boys benefit from such sources too.

Teachers often try to teach reading using fictional prose, when in fact brain research and assessment results confirm that diverse learners need diverse materials and may learn better from technical materials, nonfiction, visual media, graphics, and other resources. What you teach students to read and respond to in written form (including graphical) is at least as important as getting them to engage in literacy tasks in the first place. Try this strategy: Over the course of a week in your classroom, use Table 7.5 or a similar chart to record how much time you spend using different kinds of media each day.

The academic achievement gap between white students and students from other racial and ethnic groups grows as students progress through the grades. Elementary teachers need to differentiate for their youngest learners. Closing the learning gap means using what we know and making substantial changes in what we prioritize to teach and the materials with which we choose to teach.

Table 7.5   Time spent reading different types of materials (minutes per day)

	Monday	Tuesday	Wednesday	Thursday	Friday
Fiction—Prose					
Fiction—Verse					
Nonfiction—Text based					
Documents—Charts, graphs, maps, etc.					
Computer-based material					
Quantitative material					

LIFELONG LEARNER ORIENTATION

By the time you read this text, there probably will be new international jobs that none of us had heard of when we wrote this text. The latest computer chip designs will change, user interfaces will get more sophisticated, and voice recognition software will inch ever closer to realistic workplace applications.

Innovative Literacy Skills

How does the rapidly expanding pace of change in technology, information, and knowledge impact elementary school learning? The International Center for Leadership in Education conducted a study of workplace documents and college-level texts and materials (Daggett, 2003a). Each had specialized vocabulary and organization, but the readability levels of both were remarkably similar. Put in classroom terms, if the complexity of the average workplace e-mail directive or handbook is as complex as a college text, what literacy skills should elementary teachers emphasize?

Schools that employ the narrow use of fictional materials and writing assignments in the elementary grades will *not* produce lifelong learners as often as schools where young students have a balance of instructional materials. The innovative skills today's learners need include the following (Daggett, 2003b):

- The ability to move easily between various resources
- The ability to work with one or more people to interpret and use documents, resources, verbal explanations, and other sources
- The ability to anticipate the type of information they will need in particular situations
- The ability to read, interpret, analyze, and use a variety of documents
- The ability to respond to various forms of directions and perform the required steps or actions
- The ability to access information efficiently
- The ability to have a transferable speaking, writing, reading, and listening vocabulary across sources to make rapid connections

Students who can fluidly switch between all kinds of text, writing, and verbal language input will clearly do better at learning new job skills over the course of their lives.

Proficiency Using Prose, Document, and Quantitative Literacies

We read to comprehend text; we are literate when we have the ability to solve everyday problems that require us to use information and ideas from a variety of sources. In an International Reading Study conducted by the Educational Testing Service (ETS) in 2000, the results showed that adept readers were able to use graphic organizers to find information and draw conclusions, perform certain tasks as a result of reading, solve stated problems, realize the limitations of information, or spot missing information. ETS determined that "the level of prose, document, and quantitative literacy is a powerful predictor of how well one does in the labor market" (Sum, Kirsch, & Taggart, 2002, p. 6).

Reviewing NAEP assessment data for the year 2000, Coley (2002) noted that although 63% of fourth graders could read at a basic level, only 32% were proficient. Based on that research from ETS and NAEP then, proficient learners are learners who can do the following:

- Go beyond basic understanding
- Extend ideas
- Make inferences
- Draw conclusions
- Make connections with their own experiences

Students need to achieve proficiency in these skills across three major types of reading: prose, document, and quantitative information. Compared with other nations, the United States does not score very well on document literacy, but it is imperative that our young learners acquire proficiency in working with visual representations like charts, graphs, maps, and diagrams. These skills enable learners to think in terms of practical applications of multidimensional information as they develop innovative solutions to new and increasingly complex problems.

Students need to receive learning strategies and materials that promote prose, document, and quantitative literacies. For example, a science unit that includes an experiment could conclude with a reflective thinking organizer that allows students to demonstrate their learning through multiple representations (see Table 7.6). Interpreting documents and performing complex quantitative tasks have high payoffs in closing the learning gap and in the future work potential of diverse learners (Barton, 2003).

PRACTICAL AND ADAPTIVE THINKING

Our innovative student of the twenty-first century needs to be able to respond to real-life situations. Student will be consumers, workers, and family members, and they will need to adapt to the daily changes these roles bring. Students will need to be good at adapting to new information or interactions, making decisions and plans, and self-selecting actions, beliefs, and interpersonal responses.

Table 7.6   Reflecting on science using prose, document, and quantitative literacy together

What happened in this experiment? Diagram or draw it and label the steps or parts.	How could it be done differently? Use an example from your own experience. Do a quick write.	Create a way to graph this information. Describe why you chose this graphing method below, then create your graph on another piece of paper and attach it.

Integrated Curriculum

Getting students off to a good start at the elementary level requires us to use various forms of scenario-based learning as we integrate literacy and content for productive reasoning. To create integrated approaches to curriculum, however, we need to be selective about what we teach.

Robert Marzano (2004) tells us that if we were to teach all of the standards required in national and state standards documents, we would have to change schooling from K–12 to K–22. He goes on to say that there are the following:

- 255 standards across 14 subject areas
- 3,500 benchmarks
- 13,000 hours of class time available
- 9,000 hours of instruction time available
- 15,500 hours of instruction needed to cover the 3,500 benchmarks

So, how do we prioritize our curriculum? Establishing our focus through a lens that takes into account what our students need for practical and adaptive thinking for lifelong learning, across subject areas as well as in the workplace, should help guide the choices we make. Marzano (2004) talks about a "viable and guaranteed curriculum with challenging goals and feedback" (p. 15). Students need not only to read, write, listen, and speak, but also to observe and do them during every unit. Practical and adaptive thinking require rehearsal, practice, and celebration of success whenever the students have solved real and challenging problems.

Learning Activities

Learning activities can be designed to give students opportunities to practice these essential skills frequently and with growing finesse. The best methods use realistic scenarios and interactive activities (see Table 7.7), they help students practice preplanning and flexibility in the use of resources (see Figure 7.1), and they help students celebrate their successes in ways that promote future planning and future successes (see Figure 7.2). Rehearsing planning and celebrating real and challenging problem solving helps students develop a practical and adaptive use of information (Andres & Lupart, 1993). This will benefit learners not only when they reach the workplace, but it can also be about successful relationships and life choices, enhancing their lives both present and future.

Speaking about teaching science, Einstein (n.d.) once said:

The mere formulation of a problem is often far more essential than its solution, which may be merely a matter of mathematical or experimental skills. To raise new questions, new possibilities, to regard old problems from a new angle requires creative imagination and marks real advances in science.

Prioritizing instructional, learning, curriculum, and assessment for practical and adaptive thinking has high payoff for lifelong learning.

Table 7.7   Key scenario-based learning strategies for practical and adaptive thinking

Action Required	Literacy Strategy	Targeted Thinking
Comparing and Contrasting	• Graphic organizer use • Use of consumer-based documents • Interpersonal situation role-plays	Interpretation and prioritization
Classifying	• Sorting tray • Charting • Pattern-based activities with manipulatives • Lists • Semantic feature analysis	Comparison of attributes and generalization
Solving Problems	• Written analysis • Diagram or web • Question development • Debates • Mock trials • The Dragon Is Sleeping (see Figure 7.2)	Evaluation of solutions and self-evaluation of performance
Experimentation	• Science lab • Role-plays • Use of a variety of math strategies • Use of color or sound to convey meaning	Inquiry, risk taking, purposeful selection of strategies
Construction of Meaning	• Persuasive writing • Script development • Projects • Multimedia presentation • Simulations • Jigsaw activities • Mini-society	Adaptive reasoning, parts-to-whole relationships, schema development, detection of bias and assumptions
Planning	• Before and after pictures • Flowchart • Journey map • Story or project map • How-to handbook • Odyssey of the mind • The Shopping Cart (see Figure 7.1)	Anticipation of needs, sequential thought, noting consequences, influencing outcomes, and self-reflection (celebration)

INFLUENTIAL COMMUNICATION

One of the most significant forms of writing that promotes innovative literacy is persuasive writing (see Chapter 5 for a fuller discussion). Stating and researching a claim, using evidence, and drawing logical yet creative solutions require every form of literacy we have described. Persuasion is often the cumulative effect of literate reasoning. We must assimilate

Figure 7.1   Loading the shopping cart

Directions: Students use a shopping cart to gather the resources they will need to complete a project or reach a goal. This is like going to the grocery store to get the ingredients for a meal. If you forget one ingredient, your meal will not be complete, or the taste will be affected.

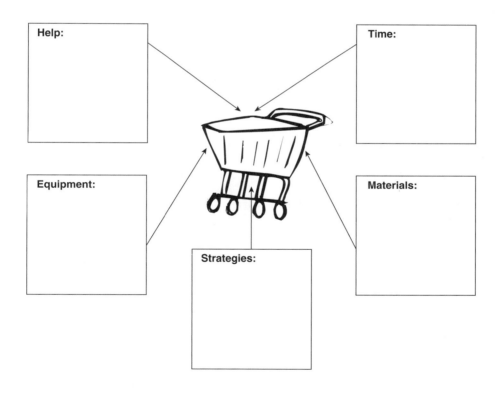

Figure 7.2   The dragon is sleeping

What was my success?

What made it hard to solve my problem? (What dragons were in my path?)

What did I do to get rid of the roadblocks? (How did I make the dragons sleep so I could reach success?)

information, form questions, draw conclusions, and then pose possibilities from our conclusions.

Most of us learn to draw logical conclusions when we write to persuade, but this is still *insufficient* for the kind of innovative literacy we are discussing here. Here we are talking about drawing logical and *innovative* conclusions to become truly *adept* communicators, ready for twenty-first century challenges. Check your rubrics and scoring guides: Do you ask for innovation when you ask learners for solutions? Do you model innovation in your exemplar papers? What you ask for from students and what you model for students is what you get from them.

Persuasion, Influence, and Ethics

Learning to leverage influence begins through understanding others' persuasive communications. Studying advertising and sales, and sorting out their messages, can help students become critical consumers of what persuasive personalities and approaches offer.

The thinking behind persuasion must be taught, and it is important that teachers include influence and ethics among its attributes. Such attributes include:

- Detection of bias
- Determining point of view
- Determining what is ethical
- Evaluating the completeness of a problem statement
- Determining beliefs and ethics of self and speakers
- Determining the source for the conclusions drawn by self and others
- Evaluating the pros and cons of solutions and claims
- Determining what information may be missing or incomplete

Examples of ways to teach these things include comparing two speeches and determining the attributes of each argument and conclusion. Giving a speech with a purposeful omission can allow students to detect the error. Fairy tales and well-known stories are good sources of materials for studying persuasion, as are Internet ads, current events, and television commercials.

Sources of material can be spoken, written, or multimedia. The analysis process used across all of these media can be a good way to develop generalized skills in evaluating persuasive messages and practicing ethical and influential communications that go beyond simple persuasion. Paul and Elder (2003) maintain that "all reasoning is based on assumptions or beliefs that we take for granted" (p. 41). Innovative and influential reasoning must be clear, justifiable, and consistent with fact and principles or beliefs. Even young learners need to be taught the following:

- How to recognize and be clear about the assumptions they make
- How to give evidence for logical and creative conclusions and claims
- How to demonstrate consistency in the use of facts and recognition of beliefs (Paul and Elder, 2003)

Learning how to speak persuasively, influentially, and ethically will help students get their needs and wants met as adults.

HIGH PAYOFF FOR THE UNKNOWN FUTURE

Students and adults who achieve proficiency in innovative literacy demonstrate a few interesting characteristics. They are creative in terms of originality, purpose, mobility, and intrinsic motivation (Perkins, 1984). These are people who consider possibilities, tolerate ambiguity, challenge the norm, look for evidence on all sides of an argument, and revise their goals when needed (Glatthorn & Baron, 1985). Innovative people ask questions, frame and reframe problems, and imagine possibilities. They seek to work at or beyond their current capacity rather than remain with the comfort of the ordinary.

Both elementary and secondary students need high-payoff rehearsals in all aspects of innovative literacy. The College Board tells us that if we are to get more underrepresented populations ready for advanced classes or post-secondary options, teacher must focus on the following:

1. Providing all students with complex, meaningful problems in the curriculum

2. Providing meaningful tasks that connect students' life experiences and cultures with school

3. Employing new instructional strategies that put students in active, problem-solving roles

4. Making discussion and student-generated questions the medium for learners

5. Embedding basic skills instruction within more complex contexts (Building Success, 2003, p. 8.3)

Teachers who give young learners opportunities to rehearse and practice the skills of innovative literacy will benefit both inside the classroom and out. These concepts will help our students encounter family, work, entertainment, financial issues, and other ordinary dilemmas with a greater sense of self and a larger repertoire of creative solution–oriented thinking skills. Innovative literacy will help our current students prepare for an unknown future of possibilities.

Managing Instruction in the Differentiated Literacy Classroom 8

What future do you envision for your students? Does the future of which you dream include meaningful work and rewarding relationships? Do you worry about a future that includes dead ends and unhappy interactions? Teachers can offer students three essential gifts that last a lifetime:

1. The first gift is that of personal regard, with respect shown in all interactions with students. The single most influential thing a teacher can do is form a mutually meaningful relationship with a student.

2. The second most important gift is that of thinking. This includes challenging and varied work that engages the student and requires increasing levels of critical thought.

3. The third gift for our students is that of literacy. Literacy allows students to become lifelong learners and increases the probability of a rewarding future.

We conclude this book with a view of reality. Elementary teachers have a tough job. Managing and planning for the needs of diverse learners is not a simple task. In this chapter, we want to offer you tools to assist you with the following:

- Unit planning for literacy learning: methods of planning and integration with templates and sample units for grades K–6. We have too much to teach, and this method helps us focus on what is truly important
- Managing literacy instruction in diverse classrooms: ideas and strategies for managing complex classrooms, with the organizational tools and supportive structures that will help you plan and differentiate your units and lessons
- Strategies for learners with difficulties: methods and tools that help with students who may have common literacy problems
- Developing independent learners: methods of helping students attain the level of independence they will need for true success

UNIT PLANNING FOR LITERACY LEARNING

Creating a preferable future for our students starts with good planning and anticipation of student needs. It also means that teachers collect and use data to make decisions about which strategies will work for which students under which circumstances. This type of diagnostic thinking is essential for classrooms where the literacy levels vary with each individual student. Unit planning for literacy learning starts with standards and then incorporates materials, concepts, questions, assessments, literacies, key skills, learner needs, and learner profiles (see Figure 8.1)

Grades K–1 (Table 8.1)

Table 8.1 offers a literacy unit for Grades K–1. The teacher can further customize the unit through grouping strategies and choice of materials. Varying group configurations could allow for individual rehearsal, practice in pairs, or critical thinking in small groups or the whole group.

Brain research tells us that the brain loves patterns, and teachers could try adding songs or music as a differentiation strategy. Learners could start with a song like "Row, row, row your boat" and change the words to "Fly, fly, fly your plane." This could allow students to compare and contrast as

Figure 8.1   Deciding what to teach and how to plan your unit using literacy

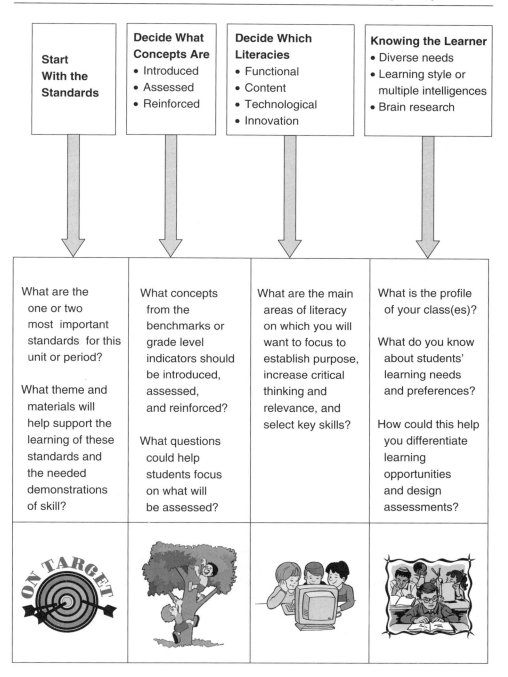

well as get the big idea of the song, staying consistent with the big idea as they add newer ideas.

Grades 2–3 (Table 8.2)

Ideas that can help teachers add differentiation to this unit include the following:

- Using personal relationships to discover new information that is respectful of learners who come from diverse social, cultural, and economic backgrounds
- Using graphic organizers to encourage deeper thinking
- Using a student self-assessment checklist or a student-friendly rubric for oral and multimedia reports

Web sites that can help you with ideas and planning include *www .lauracandler.com* and *www.TeachingMadeEasier.com.* For just $2.00 per month, you can subscribe to this site that allows you to customize your own activities and games around your specific reading, math, and science vocabulary words. For a wonderful resource for help in creating materials for ESL and bilingual students, try downloading the template at *www.readingAtoZ.com.* The template will generate word searches, lists, crossword puzzles, and games in English and several other languages.

Grades 5–6 (Table 8.3)

Ideas for adding differentiation to this unit include the following:

- Ordering scripts from television programs or tapes for viewing
- Teaching the math required by the standards and then collaborating with the art teacher to create the model. If the art teacher is unwilling, or if time is too limited, students can explore design elements on the Internet or in the library. That may mean using a two-dimensional graphed model with labels instead of the three-dimensional model. The same concepts can still be taught, although the three-dimensional nature of geometry will not be reinforced as well
- Stressing accuracy of calculation in math but then moving to understanding and acting on complex problem directions, working in a group, or giving the students challenges that promote adaptive and flexible thinking in mathematics

Table 8.4 offers a template that teachers can use for their own standards-based unit planning.

Table 8.1 Unit planning to focus learning for results: reading, writing, and speaking; Grades K–1

Grades: K–1	Time of Year	Teacher or Team	Subject Areas
	Week 2 and 3 of school year for first grade Second semester for K	Kindergarten and first grade art, music, library, and specialized teachers	Reading, writing, handwriting, spelling, library, art, and music
Standards • Reading a variety of materials • Reading, writing, and speaking for a variety of purposes	**Key Concepts** *Introduce* Consonant and rhyming word families *Assess* Speaking, reading, writing, and rhyming words *Reinforce* • Phonological awareness • Phonemics • Spelling	**Literacies** ❏ Functional • Oral language development • Phonological awareness • Phonemics • Spelling and early writing • Meaning ❏ Content area • Schema • Asking questions ❏ Innovative • Creativity • Adaptive reasoning	**Knowing the Learners** *Diverse needs or groups* 8 successful readers 12 emergent or readiness level readers—6 are ELL 2 fluent readers 8 Special Education (6 linguistic, 1 behavioral, 1 multicategorical) Mixed socioeconomic and ethnic Even mix of boys and girls *Multiple intelligence factors and brain research* More visual and kinesthetic learners than auditory and linguistic

A Theme for This Unit: Fun With Words: Nursery Rhymes and Poetry
Time: 2 weeks
Schedule: During literacy, music, art, and library

Reading Source and Genre Ideas	Critical Questions	Skill Statements	Strategies
Poetry Nursery rhymes Multicultural examples **Focus for Writing** Word families Rhyme completion Prewriting pictures **Focus for Speaking and Listening** Songs Poems Rhymes	• Do I know what rhyming words look like and how to sound them out? • Can I read and say words that rhyme? • Can I write and draw words that rhyme? • Do I know what songs and poems are about?	Students will practice rhymes to learn consonants and word families. Students will recognize, say, and write beginning and ending sounds and selected consistent vowel patterns. Students will be able to describe or draw the main idea of a poem, rhyme, or song. **Relevance** Learning songs and poems from different cultures helps us enjoy our differences.	*All* • Leveled reading materials • Matching for same and different *Emergent readers/ELL/auditory* • Whole Group: Songs and choral reading with actions • Pairs: Think-pair-share, then draw and write • Construct new parts to rhymes, songs, or poems *Visual Learners* • Mind map • Word organizers • Word wall **Assessment** Alone: • Word family books • Read a new poem or rhyme using phonics strategies Small group: Recite a poem or rhyme Pairs: Tell what your rhyme is about

Table 8.2   Unit planning to focus learning for results: social studies literacy, Grades 2–3

Grades 2–3	Time of Year	Teacher or Team	Subject Areas
	Fourth quarter or spring	Second and third grade teachers, librarians, specialized teachers	Literacy, library, social studies, computer lab
Standard • Read, speak, and write for a variety of purposes and audiences. ***American Library Association Standard*** • The student who is information literate evaluates information critically and competently	**Key Concepts** ***Introduce*** Main idea ***Assess*** Relevant and nonrelevant information ***Reinforce*** Fact versus opinion Verify sources	**Literacies** ***Functional Literacy*** Meaning ***Content Literacy*** Vocabulary Schema development Question formation ***Technological Literacy*** Questioning authority Production	**Knowing the Learners** • Many visual learners • 3 ELL & 6 IEPs • More boys than girls • 2 gifted readers and writers • Poverty level varies

A Theme for this Unit: What makes people live in certain places? (Grades 3–6)
Time: 2 weeks
Schedule: During literacy, computer lab, library, and social studies

Reading Source Ideas	Critical Questions	Skill Statements	Strategies
• National Geographic World & other age-appropriate print and Internet periodicals • Government Web sites with statistics • Stories of immigrants • Native Americans' daily lives **Focus for Writing** Expository—writing to provide information **Focus for Speaking and Listening** • Interviewing • Reporting	• How could we search for information about where people live? • What information is important? What are the main ideas I want people to know about?	• Students will use multiple sources for research to determine good sources and key information • Students will be able to verify and substantiate fact versus opinion **Relevance** How did my family end up in our town and in this neighborhood? What factors in choosing where to live would I want to consider?	***Boys/IEPs/ELL/Visual Learners*** • Graphic organizers • Note taking tools • Internet access ***GT/All*** • Choice in reading materials • Centers ***Poverty/All*** • Rehearsal for center behaviors • Interview parents and grandparents or other favorite people **Assessments** • Note taking of relevant information • Graphic organizer fact versus opinion • Written report for final assessment • Oral, multimedia reports

Table 8.3   Unit planning to focus learning for results: mathematics literacy, Grades 5–6

Grades 5–6	Time of Year	Teacher or Team	Subject Areas
	Fourth quarter or spring	Fifth and sixth grade teachers, specialized teachers (may be math teachers)	Literacy Math
Standard • Students will use mathematical concepts to solve complex problems • Students will communicate their mathematical thinking and adaptive reasoning • Students will read, write, and speak for a variety of purposes and audiences	**Key Concepts** ***Introduce*** Adaptive reasoning for three-dimensional geometry ***Assess*** Solve and explain complex space and area problems ***Reinforce*** Procedural math (calculation) Sequential writing in math Noting details	**Literacies** ***Functional Literacy*** Meaning—details and literal information ***Content Literacy*** Text orientation Vocabulary Expository writing Problem solving Making connections ***Technological Literacy*** Demystifying directions Media orientation ***Innovative Literacy*** Flexible and adaptive thinking	**Knowing the Learners** Highly multicultural, average level of poverty 60% females 4 ELL 35% below proficiency in reading 65% below proficiency in writing Highly verbal learners and average visual learners Average number of special education and gifted learners

A Theme for This Unit: ***Trading Spaces*** (Take-off from the cable television show)
Time: 2 weeks
Schedule: During literacy, art, and math

Reading Source Ideas	Critical Questions	Skill Statements	Strategies ***Verbal Studies/Diverse Ethnic and Economic Backgrounds***
Geometry problems Scripts Product labels **Focus for Writing** Scripting Directions	• How do I use what I know about the elements of design to create a comfortable space for a friend? • How will I use what I know about estimation,	• Students use multiple ways to calculate area and perimeter • Students use appropriate tools to measure walls, floors, ceilings, and furnishings	• Survey and interview my *Trading Spaces* partners • Summarize their preferences for comfortable spaces in their house or apartment • Script and television as a motivator and reinforcement for all forms of literacy

(Continued)

Table 8.3 (Continued)

Focus for Speaking and Listening *Trading Spaces* television program	calculation, and problem solving to save money on remodeling? • How will I record the progress of the project and explain my process to others?	• Students create an accurate and labeled scale model of a house or selected rooms • Students develop a script to explain the process for redecorating a friend's space **Relevance** People try to create comfortable spaces, and they have to maintain their environment	***Visual Learners/Limited English or Literacy Abilities*** • Math and art tools • Art elements of design—multicultural examples • Hands-on learning through measurement and models **Assessments** • Use graph paper to draw spaces and calculate the amount of carpet and paint needed to redecorate on a budget • Create a three-dimensional model of a space using design elements from art and accurate scaled calculations in math • Write a script to describe the process used to create the space and the satisfaction of the people for whom it was created

MANAGING LITERACY INSTRUCTION IN DIVERSE CLASSROOMS

So, your classroom has twenty-seven students, and you want to do an oral reading assessment that must be administered individually, or you want to run six groups of students in flexible groups for language arts. The big question is: how do you manage an environment where multiple activities are occurring simultaneously?

Throughout this book, including the previous section on unit planning, we have been giving you examples of good strategies for managing instruction in complex classrooms. We've been assuming that certain basics are

Table 8.4   Standards-based unit planning guide for literacy learning: template for Grades K–6

Grade	Time of Year	Teacher or Team	Subject Areas
Standards	**Key Concepts** *Introduce* *Assess* *Reinforce*	**Literacies** ❑ Functional Literacy ❑ Content Literacy ❑ Technological Literacy ❑ Innovative Literacy	**Knowing the Learners:** Diverse needs or groups Learning style/ multiple intelligence factors/brain research

A Theme for This Unit:

Time:

Schedule:

Reading Source and Genre Ideas	Critical Questions	Skill Statements	Strategies
Reading Source and Genre Ideas **Focus for Writing** **Focus for Speaking and Listening**		 **Relevance**	 **Assessments**

already in place: class rules are understood, rehearsed, and reinforced. Rituals and routines are modeled and practiced at regular intervals. A well-run classroom is like an enduring play: it has classic elements and appeal, and it is engaging and well-rehearsed.

The purpose for following such routines should be a gradual increase in learner autonomy. Students love choice and seek independence, so this should be a natural consequence of good behavior. Students who comply with rules can earn certain rights and freedoms, such as movement around the room, work in alternative areas, choice of communication methods, use of special tools (e.g., colored pencils, computers), and other desirable choices. A classroom climate that supports students through earned autonomy can mitigate students' negative attitudes toward learning (McNeeley, Nonnemaker, & Blum, 2002), and accelerate their learning at the same time.

Diverse Learners With Diverse Organizational Skills

The interesting thing about organization is that it is learned, cultural, and often dependent on wealth and well-being. Students of poverty rarely have enough resources to worry about organization. Instead, the chaos of unknown forces shaking their world is a source of ongoing stress. Students with certain kinds of disabilities are prone to disorganized methods of accessing the world, have difficulties using resources designed for learners with full abilities, and can't find tools that work well for them.

Students from other cultures may have been exposed to methods of organization that are more or less formal than those of schools in this country. Coming to the United States and not being able to speak the language upsets patterns of organization and predictability in many ways because basic classroom communication contains many elements and clues to expected organization and structure. Certain gifted and talented learners do not always see the importance or relevance of organization, especially with regard to topics or items for which they have no interest or connection.

One of the greatest gifts a teacher can give students is the ability to organize their environment at school. Using nonverbal clues; modeling and rehearsing putting away and finding strategies; color; special containers; folders; and other resources can be extremely helpful, but only if they are taught, rehearsed, and reinforced.

Students who can be taught how to develop a plan, prioritize, schedule, and self-talk their way through life can access any type of learning more easily. Students don't always come to us with these skills. The skills they bring to school allow them to survive outside of school (Payne, 2001), but teachers who assume students come with the ability to follow directions, think in a step-by-step fashion, and understand the consequences of chaos do students a disservice. Teachers must model these techniques by talking out loud about logical steps in thinking, demonstrating how to plan and schedule, and offering their students choices and goals they can use with their own organizational methods.

Simultaneous Learning Activities

Once a classroom's behavioral and organizational norms have been established and practiced, what is next? We recommend the following strategies for helping teachers manage diverse classroom activities occurring at the same time. These strategies can work wonders at the elementary level:

- Menus
- Centers
- Class space
- Flexible grouping
- Parent or community volunteers
- Questioning
- Adjustable assignments
- Student learning contracts

Table 8.5 offers good ways to get started with these strategies. By learning even one of these techniques well, it will be easier for you to manage a literacy-based classroom with multiple activities going on at once. We'll use centers as an example and develop that for you in more depth.

CENTERS

Centers are wonderful ways to build self-reliance and differentiate for diverse learners. They allow students to work in areas of their strengths or multiple intelligences or perhaps stretch in an area that still has room for growth.

Centers provide choice, novelty, reinforcement, and opportunities for independent and collaborative application and practice (active processing). They can be set up for remediation or enrichment depending on what students need. They can be open-ended or prescriptive in their design. They are generally organized around the room with tables, counters, floor space, or wall space designated for each particular center.

Table 8.5 Attributes of strategies to manage diverse literacy activities

Menus/Choice Boards	Centers
• Equal options, watch your verbs and vocabulary to stay equal • Reinforce higher levels of critical thinking • Choice is limited or unrestricted depending on student data • Don't use for every assignment • Establish a method of selection and approval for the selection • Use models and scoring guides to help students self-evaluate	• Rules or guidelines are rehearsed • Provide models of the desired result at centers where possible • Use investigations and problem solving frequently at centers • Introduce to the whole group with expectations and routines • Use technology where applicable • Establish personal goal setting and student self-evaluation • Sequential, topical, thinking, or product dependent
Student Learning Contracts	**Flexible Groups**
• Aspects of communication method, time, and resources are listed • Purpose is specific to learning or project • Students can negotiate established aspects of learning • Can be written, or create a choice board and students can move name into choices • Both parties must agree • Resources can be people or things or places	• Organize by learning style, need, or content, but not by "life sentence" • Students know the purpose of the group and desired result • Students know how and when groups change • Students have self-selection opportunities as a reward or when appropriate to the learning • Students can self-evaluate their way into a particular group
Parents and Other Volunteers	**Use of Classroom Space**
• Clear directions oral and written • Rehearsed actions with students • Oversight and reinforcement • Vocabulary or key word sheet provided specific to the assignment • Models and scoring guides are helpful, watching you do it first • Special place for individual or group work with a volunteer • Rituals for thanking and appreciating any and all contributions	• Areas for reading, writing, and quiet partner work • Areas for assessment • Areas for group work • Lighting and decoration make things more inviting • Special furnishings where permitted: sack chairs, cushions, lamps • Special tools that can never leave the area • Tools and furnishings that are portable
Adjustable or Tiered Assignments	**Questions and Prompts**
• Specific to the level of student per assessment results • Equivalent in content, but may be diverse in product or process • Students assigned to group or assignment • Practice for specific skills and thinking given • Resources may vary by assignment type • Questions or prompts may vary	• Use of questions to differentiate homework and other assignments • Vary prompts by learner style or need • Create questions ahead of a discussion that vary in critical thinking level, and ask students through specific selection method • Student formation of questions also allows a form of differentiation • Use of personal goal statements as starting points for question formation and investigation

Questions teacher often ask about centers include the following:

- How do I move students to centers?
- How do I assign or let students select the centers they work in?
- How do I oversee center work when I can't be everywhere?

Centers should be designed with the "end in mind." They should be not just activities but intentional learning experiences based on learning standards and student needs. If the centers are well designed, thoughtfully constructed, interesting, and engaging, there is less chance for students to become disruptive and waste time. When students are working at meaningful, useful tasks in centers, the teacher can be freed up to work with a small group for a separate mini-lesson or a guided reading situation. Perfect orchestration doesn't happen on the first attempt, as students need time to become accustomed to the freedom of working in the centers and develop the self-monitoring to work without direct teacher supervision.

Centers may be used for social studies, science, health, or other content areas. They facilitate opportunities to read, write, talk, and listen in any discipline, allowing for vocabulary development, construction of meaning of new ideas and concepts, self-monitoring, collaborative social growth, skill development, and application of information in practical, analytical, and creative ways (Sternberg, 1998). Table 8.6 offers examples of twelve centers appropriate for elementary classrooms.

Center Selection and Grouping

Many teachers let students select the centers that appeal to them. They may use a contract and sign up for one or two centers to work in for a few days or a week. Some teachers set up a rotation chart and post it so students can see which center they are in on which day.

Clothespin grouping is a convenient way to help sort students to different centers (see Table 8.7). On a chart (or portable whiteboard) list your criteria for grouping. Use clothespins with students' names on them and clip the appropriate name to the selected criteria. Here are some examples:

- Choice of topic or prompt
- Choice of question to address or choice of problem
- Assignment completion
- Center for the day

Students take the clothespin with their names and select the center they want to work in. If the teacher limits the number in each group,

Table 8.6   Sample centers

Poets Corner: Students create poetry alone or with partners. Different types of poetry forms may be suggested or required. Samples of each type may be displayed so students have a model. It may be that students read poetry for enjoyment as well.	**Author's Corner:** Students are able to get to know authors better. There may be a variety of resources at their disposal. They may write letters or send e-mails to authors, sharing what they liked about the book or any questions they may have.
Colorful Words: Using pocket charts or white boards, students may create vocabulary lists to use in their writing, using feeling words and descriptive language connected to a topic they are writing about	**Storyboards:** Students may create storyboard pictures to show the sequence of the story. These can be displayed with text added underneath to tell the story.
Word Wizards: Students work with magnetic, sandpaper, or felt letters to create spelling words. For tactile learners this is a way of feeling and using more sensory memory.	**Listening Center:** Students use earphones to listen to recorded readings. They may read along or just follow the text. This is especially helpful in developing fluency and voice in readers.
Artist Loft: A variety of media is available for students to use to create visuals that represent favorite passages or events from their reading. Pastels, crayon, paint, markers, and construction paper may be available for their use. There may be a collaborative mural to which students add over time.	**Pen Pals:** Students may write to other children in other classrooms about their reading. They may be partnered with another school in a near or far place to make writing more relevant and meaningful. This could be done in the Technology Center using e-mail.
Newspaper Reporter: A class newspaper may be published for parents and others in the school. Short articles on topics of interest or student book reviews may be produced. Using a computer publishing program may be a new technology skill to develop.	**Technology Center:** The possibilities are endless. Students may publish their own stories. They may use Kidspiration or Inspiration Software to create graphics that display characterization or plot and theme and sequence of events in the story. They may use the Internet to access information they need on a particular topic.
Theater Center: Students may create skits or short plays that retell a story they have read. They may create a play and then write it out for others to read. Puppets and felt boards work well as a variation on this theme. Costumes may be available for their use. Digital cameras are used to record their tableaus, and then they create a booklet where they are in the illustrations.	**Cool Stuff:** This center may have interesting materials, such as gel pens, glitter markers, and paper with interesting borders where students might create advertising flyers for the books they have read. There may be shape books that can be used to write about a topic that intrigues them. Flip-up books, mobiles, and pop-up books may be created.

Table 8.7   Clothespin board for organizing groups

_____ **Center:**	_____ **Center:**
_____ **Center:**	_____ **Center:**
_____ **Center:**	_____ **Center:**

students will then clip their clothespin to the center that indicates their second choice. The teacher may also assign students to the center based on learning needs or appropriate lesson sequence.

Teachers can organize student center assignments for the full week by using an organizer like the one shown in Table 8.8. The chart may be set

Table 8.8   Teacher organizer for assigning students to centers

Center	Monday	Tuesday	Wednesday	Thursday	Friday
Poets' Center					
Authors' Center					
Colorful Words					
Storyboards					
Pen Pals					

up as a pocket chart or as a bulletin board so that names of centers and students assigned to them may be easily viewed or changed. The number of centers set up depends on available space, skills development, and targeted standards. The centers may change each week for variety and a different focus. In that case the names of the centers would change on the pocket chart and so forth.

Managing Student Work in Centers

Post the Directions

Teachers also may post the activities or routines clearly visible in the center so students can refer to the directions without running to the teacher. We have to remember that students do not have limitless memory spaces in their short-term working memory and may need to refer to the directions when they need them rather than trying to remember what the teacher said twenty minutes earlier. This will make the work go more smoothly and help students become more self-directed.

Organize the Materials

Teachers need to organize materials and resources to facilitate the orderliness of the center and help students access what they need. Well-organized materials help to leave the center in order for the next group. Items for a particular center may be color coded so that if they get moved children know where they belong. Plastic tubs and milk cartons will hold books, magazines, and other such things that students may need. Tote boxes with lids are good for holding pens, pencils, markers, stickers, and other neat stuff.

Assigning Roles

Students in the center may choose roles to manage the centers. Suggestions for roles such as material manager, timekeeper, technician, and facilitator may be used. The roles will depend on whether they are needed for maintenance of the center or for the collaborative process if students are to work together to accomplish a cooperative task.

Student Tracking

Students may use contracts or agendas to monitor their own center work. Table 8.9 offers a personal agenda that each student can use to organize their center work for the week, set goals, and reflect on progress.

Table 8.9   Personal center agenda

Day	Center	What I did	What I learned	Next time I . . .

Integrated Literacy Instruction

There are many ways to approach integration, and entire books have been written on the subject. There are several ways to organize the integration of literacies, and our favorite methods include the following:

- By common concepts in the grade-level standards
- The components of literacy: reading, writing, speaking, and listening
- Through the strategy selection given to students in menus, centers, or prompts
- Through the choice of content
- By offering rich and real-world problems to solve
- By offering high-level questions to answer

For additional examples, please check the integration examples in the units shown in Tables 8.1, 8.2, and 8.3 earlier in this chapter.

STRATEGIES FOR LEARNERS WITH LITERACY PROBLEMS

It is important to integrate all the forms of writing mentioned for each of the literacies. Giving students practice in all the forms of writing each week is a critical part of acquiring literacies and is essential to the growth of thinking skills. The research on the impact of writing is astounding. Doug Reeves (2000) frequently cites Virginia studies on standardized test scores increasing in every subject after writing practice has been increased across the curriculum.

Teaching a unit on storytelling, but then not returning to narrative writing practice for two months, by which time the storytelling and the reports are finished, will not help young writers and readers. Integrating both expository and narrative writing across the curriculum and using both forms of writing each week will help. Such integration is essential to improving the rate of growth in writing, reading, and the content areas.

Teachers will encounter learners with specific writing problems:

- Resistance to writing
- Lacks background for the writing piece
- Needs more skills
- Can't get started
- Lacks depth in the writing
- A physical disability presents challenges

Table 8.10   Suggested solutions for writers with specific problems

Resistance to writing	Lacks background	Needs more skills	Can't get started	Lacks depth	Physical disability
• Give choice • Work with a buddy • Help model and demonstrate • Begin with illustrations	• Provide resources: technological and print • Teach access skills	• Teach brainstorming • Provide advance organizers • Model processes and provide practice • Partner with more capable writer	• Work with a partner • Provide prompts and encouragement • Divide task into manageable chunks	• Use question prompts • Review and edit with a peer. Note gaps • Provide more time to research and get more information	• Access appropriate technology: audio recording and word processing • Peer support or assistance

There are many ways teachers can offer students solutions to these writing problems and needs, as detailed in Table 8.10. Specific reading needs, problems, and competencies can also be accommodated in many different ways, as shown in Figure 8.2, which covers eight different kinds of readers:

- Emerging readers
- Those who read one word at a time
- Cautious readers
- Uninterested readers
- Capable readers
- Auditory readers
- Silent readers
- Comprehending readers

DEVELOPING INDEPENDENT LEARNERS

The goal of all literacy programs is to create independent readers, writers, speakers, and listeners. Students who are independent are easier to manage in a diverse classroom with multiple tasks occurring simultaneously. To function independently, students must learn to self-evaluate, and

Figure 8.2   Suggestions for unique readers

Emerging Reader
- Expressing joy
- Print rich
- Decoding
- Word attack skills
- Reading buddy
- Computer and technology
- Choice or interest
- Label objects
- Word walls
- Oral or written
- Taped read-along

One Word at a Time
- Say word for them
- Build sight words
- Word families
- Word or letter connect
- Explicit vocabulary before reading
- Taped read-along
- Reading buddies
- Model punctuation
- Repetition

Cautious Reader
- Short assignments
- Provide success
- Level questions
- Specific praise and feedback
- Showcase talents
- Tap into multiple intelligences

Uninterested Reader
- Nonthreatening
- Model
- High interest or variety
- Choices
- Surveys
- Choice boards
- Contracts
- Rewards and incentives
- Buddy reading

Capable Reader
- Things move too slow
- Lacks self-control
- Establish taking turns
- Listening T-chart
- Signal from teacher
- Opportunities for leadership
- Challenge
- Reading buddy

Auditory Reader
- Read aloud sessions
- Choice of materials
- Younger and older student audiences
- Private space
- Elbow pipe, read to self
- Tape stories and books for others

Silent Reader
- Opportunities for silent reading
- Tape reading
- Shared reading
- Provide purposes for oral reading
- Praise for oral reading
- Retell story
- Create questions for other readers

Comprehending Reader
- Choices
- Variety of materials and genres
- Reading-related projects
- Research
- Thought-provoking topics
- Higher-order thinking

they will need rehearsal to understand and practice learning to classroom expectations.

Learning Prompts

Predictable prompts and contracts help students acquire independence and self-management skills. Prompts can be prepared on cards for volunteers who read and work with your students. Students may also use these cards to become more independent and self-reliant in their reading and writing. The following verbal prompts help get the student thinking, predicting, sampling text, confirming, and self-correcting:

- How could you use the picture to help you?
- Put your lips and tongue in the shape of the first letter.
- How does the word begin? How does the word end?
- Say it out loud; does it make sense?
- Does that sound right? Does it fit?
- Does that look right to you?
- Skip that word and go on. Now what do you think it is?
- Have you seen that word before? Where?
- Think about a word you know that starts with the same sounds.
- Put in a word that makes sense, and go on.
- Check again please.
- I will say the word you think it is. What letters and sounds start it and end it?
- What other ways could you figure out that word?

Learning Contracts

Learning contracts are another great way to foster independence in learners. Table 8.11 is a simple contract that students may use to jot down the work that needs to be completed. Students can work on each task in the order they choose, deciding for themselves whether to tackle easy items, challenging tasks, or enjoyable tasks first. This gives the students a sense of control and satisfaction. It also teaches independence and self-directed learning, encouraging the learner to self-monitor and reflect.

Students can design their own contracts that include information about content, time, process, and demonstrations of learning. For younger students, listing or checking off choices works well in contract creation. Contracts can be used for specific units, with the teacher filling in the unit and the content choices, and students then filling in the rest of the information. Table 8.12 is an example of a contract from a genre-based unit for biographies, and Figure 8.3 offers a template that teachers can adjust for differentiating assignments.

Table 8.11   Language arts learning contract

Language Arts:

Name: _____   **Week:** _____

Spelling: _____

Reading: _____

Project: _____

Other: _____

Subject: _____

Name: _____   **Week:** _____

Spelling: _____

Reading: _____

Project: _____

Other: _____

Table 8.12   Choice-based contract example

Name:	To complete my work I will need this much time: _____ One day _____ Two days _____ Three days
Content: **For Our Biography Unit** _____ Famous Athletes _____ Heroes in History _____ Scientists & Inventors _____ Other _____ Title of My Book:	I will let others know about my book by doing the following: *(Students can list written or other projects here. They can come up with their own or select from a list.)*

Focus and Sponge Activities

Focus activities, sometimes called anchor activities by Tomlinson (2001), can be used to help students focus in at the beginning of a class: eliminating distractions, opening mental files, and capitalizing on "prime time" at the beginning of a lesson or class time. Examples of focus activities that support literacy competencies include the following:

- Reflect on your homework. What was easy for you? What was difficult? Share with your partner what help you need.
- In a "quick write," tell what happened in the chapter you read last night.
- Predict what will happen next in the story.
- Review the most interesting words in the last chapter, and substitute or give a synonym for them.
- Create a crossword puzzle with the interesting words from the chapter.
- Draw the most interesting scene in that chapter.
- Develop your agenda for today.
- Create a Jeopardy category and questions.
- Using a Venn diagram, compare and contrast the two main characters.
- Create a mind map to show the events of this chapter.
- Using an implications wheel, take the crucial event and web the implications.
- Create a timeline to show the events of the story so far.
- Draw a comic strip to show the major events so far in the story.
- If you were a reporter, what would you report about this chapter?

Figure 8.3   Learning needs contract

Learning Needs Contract

Student _____ Class/Subject _____ Date _____

Unit _____

I need these changes because _____

_____

Teacher Signature X _____ Student Signature X _____

Select the changes you need below, or create your own contract.

Communication

____ Computer use

____ Someone to write for me

____ Present my work differently. How?

_____

_____

_____

____ I want to show what I know and can do on this assignment differently, so that _____

_____

_____

_____

Time/Quantity

____ Extra time because

_____

_____

_____

____ Reduce the number of items in this assignment so that _____

_____

_____

____ Change the number of items to include or replace, because

_____

_____

_____

Materials/Resources

____ Permission to use the Internet for research

____ Other research sources or methods

_____

____ Different assessment because _____

_____

____ Different assignment because _____

_____

____ These changes in materials or resources _____

_____

_____

Source: Adapted with permission from Kuzmich (1998).

These same activities can be used as "sponges" to sop up time in a positive way when other work is finished. Some teachers post the activities on a sponge board so that students have suggestions to fill their extra time in a productive way. Students may even add an item from the sponge board to their contracts. The more choice, freedom, and control students have (Glasser, 1986), the more committed they are to their learning activities and the more self-directed they become as learners. It's never too early to start.

CLASSROOMS THAT SUPPORT DIFFERENTIATED LITERACY LEARNING

Classrooms that support literacy are easy to spot. Students are busy and engaged. Reading, writing, speaking, and listening are the major focus of each day. Caring adults connect with the young learners and help them set goals and celebrate achievements.

Classrooms like this take special preparation and management, requiring educators to have a deep understanding of literacy, a varied tool kit of strategies, a diagnostic approach to teaching and learning, and a high regard for the diversity of the learners in their classrooms. We don't mean replicating the classrooms that made us successful learners when we were younger. We mean understanding the art and craft of engaging our students in what we believe to be the highest-stakes game of the twenty-first century, literacy.

Literacy is the gateway to eliminating prejudice and inviting invention and reinvention of our lives and our students' lives. It is worth the effort to reach out to each of our students to find each one's unique path to learning to read, write, speak, and listen. This starts and ends with caring teachers who do more than care—who also meet our students' basic needs for respect and dignity.

The twenty-first century offers challenges, possibilities, and adventures we cannot even imagine, although we do know that quality instruction for early reading, writing, speaking, and listening are well-documented as critical elements in any comprehensive literacy program. Equally important is the need for our students to think and interact with what they learn, because that is what literate adults do. If you integrate the four literacies into everyday teaching and learning, and if you vary your instructional and learning techniques to meet the needs of the diverse learners in your classrooms, you will be getting your elementary students off to a great start.

References

Adams, M. J. (1990). *Beginning to read: Thinking and learning about print.* Cambridge, MA: M.I.R. Press.

Ainsworth, L. (2003). *Power standards: Identifying the standards that matter the most.* Denver, CO: Advanced Learning Press and Center for Performance Assessment.

Allington, R. L. (1983). Fluency: The neglected reading goal. *The Reading Teacher, 36,* pp. 556–561.

American Library Association. (1998). *Information literacy standards for student learning.* Chicago: Author.

Anderson, T. H., & Armbruster, B. B. (1984). Studying. In P. D. Pearson, R. Barr, M. L. Kamii, & P. Mosenthal (Eds.), *Handbook of reading research* (pp. 657–679). New York: Longman.

Andres, J., & Lupart, J. (1993). *The inclusive classroom: Educating exceptional children.* Scarbourgh, ON: Nelson Canada.

Aram, D. M., & Hall, N. E. (1989). Longitudinal follow-up of children with preschool communication disorders: Treatment implications. *School Psychology Review, 18*(4), 487–501.

Armbuster, B. B., Lehr, R., & Osborn, J. (2001). *Put reading first—the research building blocks for teaching children to read.* Washington, DC: Center for the Improvement of Early Reading.

Armstrong, T. (2003). *The multiple intelligences of reading and writing: Making the words come alive.* Alexandria, VA: Association for Supervision and Curriculum Development.

Barell, J. (2003). *Developing more curious minds.* Alexandria, VA: ASCD.

Barton, P. (2003, Spring). Reading and literacy in America. *ETS Policy Notes, 11*(2), 1–10.

Baum, R. (1990). Finishing touches—10 top programs. *Learning, 18*(6), 51–55.

Benjamin, A. (2002). *Differentiated instruction: A guide for middle and high school teachers.* Larchmont, NY: Eye on Education.

Blackburn, M. (2003). Boys and literacies: What difference does gender make? *Reading Research Quarter, 38,* 276–287.

Brashir, A. S., & Scavuzzo, A. (1992). Children with language disorders: Natural history and academic success. *Journal of Learning Disabilities, 25*(1), 53–65.

Broughton, M., & Fairbanks, C. (2003). In the middle of the middle: Seventh grade girls' literacy and identity development. *Journal of Adolescent and Adult Literacy, 46,* 426–435.

Brozo, W. (2002). *To be a boy, to be a reader, engaging teen and preteen boys in active literacy.* Newark, DE: International Reading Association.

Bruce, B. (Ed.). (2003). *Literacy in the information age: Inquiries into meaning making with new technologies.* Newark, Delaware: International Reading Association.

Bruce, B. C., & Bishop, A. P. (2002, May). Using the Web to support inquiry-based literacy development. *The Journal of Adolescent and Adult Literacy, 45*(8).

Buehl, D. (2001). *Classroom strategies for interactive learning* (2nd Ed.). Newark, DE: International Reading Association.

Building success: Strategies to prepare students for college prep and AP courses in english and social studies. (2003). New York: College Entrance Examination Board.

Burke, J. (2000). *Reading reminders.* Portsmouth, NH: Boyton-Cook.

Burke, J. (2002). *Tools for thought graphic organizers for your classroom.* Portsmouth, NH: Heinemann.

Carbo, M., Dunn, R., & Dunn, K. (1986). *Teaching students to read through their individual learning styles.* Boston, MA: Allyn & Bacon.

Carter, F., & Strickland, R. (2001). *The education of Little Tree.* Albuquerque: University of New Mexico Press.

Chapman, C., & King, R. (2003). *Differentiated instructional strategies for reading in the content areas.* Thousand Oaks, CA: Corwin Press.

Chapman, C., & King, R. (2003). *Differentiated instructional strategies for writing in the content areas.* Thousand Oaks, CA: Corwin Press.

Chomsky, N. (1957). *Syntactic structures.* The Hague, Netherlands: Mouton & Co.

Clements, S., Kolbe, K., & Villapando, E. (2000). *Do-it-yourself creative thinking.* Phoenix, AZ: Think In Publications.

Coley, R. (2002, March). An uneven start: Indicators of inequity in school readiness. In *Policy Information Report,* Policy Information Center: Educational Testing Service.

Colorado Department of Education. (2004). *Gifted and talented education.* Retrieved August 3, 2004, from http://www.cde.state.co.us/gt/

Coney, J. (1998). Hemispheric priming in a reading task. *Brain and Language, 62*(1), 34–50.

Coney, J. (2002). Probing hemispheric processes in an on-line reading task. *Brain and Language, 80*(2), 130–141.

Coney, J., & Evans, K. D. (2000). Hemispheric asymmetries in the resolution of lexical ambiguity. *Neuropsychologia, 38*(3), 272–282.

Constantino, R. (Ed.). (1998). *Literacy, access, and libraries among the language minority population.* London: The Scarecrow Press.

Council for Exceptional Children Web site. (2004). Retrieved from http://www.cec.sped.org/

Covey, S. (1989). *The seven habits of highly effective people: Restoring the character ethic.* New York: Simon and Schuster.

Cowan, G., & Cowan, E. (1980). *Writing.* New York: Wiley.

Craik, F., & Lockhart, R. (1972). Levels of processing: A framework for memory research. *Journal of Verbal Learning and Verbal Behavior, 11,* 671–684.

Crow, J., & Quigley, J. (1985). A semantic field approach to passive vocabulary acquisition for reading comprehension. *TESOL Quarterly, 19,* 497–513.

Daggett, W. (2003a). *Achieving reading proficiency for all.* Retrieved August 3, 2004, from http://www.daggett.com

Daggett, W. (2003b). School counselors and information literacy from the perspective of Willard Daggett. *Professional Counseling, 6,* 238–243.

Daniels, H. (1994). *Literature circles: Voice and choice in the student-centered classroom.* York, ME: Stenhouse.

Daniels, H., & Zemelman, S. (2004). Out with textbooks, in with learning. *Educational Leadership, 61,* 36–40.

Deporter, B., Reardon, M., & Singer-Nourie, S. (1998). *Quantum teaching.* Boston: Allyn & Bacon.

Dewey, J. (1956). *The child and the curriculum & the school and society.* Chicago: University of Chicago Press. (Original works published in 1902 and 1915)

Diamond, M., & Hopson, J. (1998). *Magic trees of the mind.* New York: Penguin.

Dowhower, S. L. (1989). Repeated reading: Research into practice. *The Reading Teacher, 42,* 502–507.

Eakle, J. (2003). A content analysis of second language research in *The Reading Teacher and Language Arts, 1990–2001. The Reading Teacher, 56,* 828–836.

Edwards, J., & Malicky, G. (1996). *Constructing meaning: Integrating elementary language arts.* Toronto, ON: International Thomson Publishing.

Einstein, A. (n.d.). *Albert Einstein quotes and quotations.* Retrieved August 6, 2004, from http://www.brainyquote.com/quotes/quotes/a/alberteins121989.html

Ellis, N. (1995). Vocabulary acquisition: Psychological perspectives. *The Language Teacher, 19*(2), 12–16.

Epstein, H. T. (1978). Growth spurts during brain development: Implications for educational policy and practices. *National Society for the Study of Education Yearbook, 77*(2), 343–370.

Frayer, D., Frederick, W., & Klausmeier, H. (1969). *A schema for testing the level of concept mastery* (Technical Report No. 16). Madison: University of Wisconsin Research and Development Center for Cognitive Learning.

Gallagher, M., & Pearson, D. (1989). *Discussion, comprehension, and knowledge acquisition in content area classrooms* (Technical Report No. 480). Washington, DC: Office of Educational Research and the Illinois University, Urbana Center for the Study of Reading in Cambridge, MA.

Gardner, H. (1983). *Frames of mind: The theory of multiple intelligences.* Boulder, CO: Perseus Books Group.

Gay, G. (2004). The importance of multicultural education. *Educational Leadership, 61,* 30–35.

Geschwind, N. (1979, September). Specializations of the human brain. *Scientific American, 23*(3), 180–199.

Given, B. (2002). *Teaching to the brain's natural learning system.* Alexandria, VA: ASCD.

Glasgow, N., & Hicks, C. (2003). *What successful teachers do: 91 research-based classroom strategies for new and veteran teachers.* Thousand Oaks, CA: Corwin Press.

Glasser, W. (1986). *Control theory in the classroom.* New York: Harper & Row.

Glatthorn, A., & Baron, J. (1985). The good thinker. In A. Costa (Ed.), *Developing minds: A resource book for teaching thinking* (pp. 49–53). Alexandria, VA: ASCD.

Gonzales, F. (1995). *Teacher content subjects to LEP students: 20 tips for teachers.* San Antonio, TX: The Intercultural Development Research Association.

Gregorc, A. (1982). *Inside styles: Beyond the basics.* Columbia, CT: Gregorc Associates.

Gregory, G. (2003). Differentiated instructional strategies in practice: Training, implementation, and supervision. Thousand Oaks, CA: Corwin Press.

Gregory, G., & Chapman, C. (2002). *Differentiating instructional strategies: One size doesn't fit all.* Thousand Oaks, CA: Corwin Press.

Gregory, G., & Kuzmich, L. (2004). *Data driven differentiation in the standards-based classroom.* Thousand Oaks, CA: Corwin Press.

Grognet, A. (2000). Your professional partner: The Center for Applied Linguistics. *ESL Magazine, 3,* 10–12.

Gross, A. (1990). *Rhetoric of Science.* Cambridge, MA: Harvard Press.

Gunning, T. G. (1998). *Assessing and correcting reading and writing difficulties.* Boston: Allyn & Bacon.

Harris, J. R. (1998). *The nature assumption: Why children turn out the way they do.* New York, The Free Press.

Harste, J. C., Short, K. D., & Burke, C. (1988). *Creating classrooms for authors: The reading-writing connection.* Portsmouth, NH: Heinemann.

Hart, B., & Risley, T. R. (1995). *Meaningful differences in the everyday experience of young American children.* Baltimore: Brookes.

Hart, L. (1975). *How the brain works: A new understanding of human learning, emotion, and thinking.* Boulder, CO: Perseus Books Group.

Harvey, S., & Goudvis, A. (1998). *Nonfiction Matters.* York, ME: Stenhouse.

Harvey, S., & Goudvis, A. (2000). *Strategies that work: Teaching comprehension to enhance understanding.* York, ME: Stenhouse.

Harwayne, S. (1992). *Lasting impressions: Weaving literature into the writing workshop.* Portsmouth, NH: Heinemann.

Head, M. H., & Readence, J. E. (1986). Anticipation guides: Meaning through prediction. In E. K. Dishner, T. W. Bean, J. E. Readence, & D. W. Moore (Eds.), *Reading in the content areas: Improving classroom instruction* (1992, 3rd ed.). Dubuque, IA: Kendall/Hunt Publishing Company.

Healy, J. (1992). *Endangered minds: Why our children don't think.* New York: Simon & Schuster.

Henkelman, R. G. (1969). A neurological-impress method of remedial-reading instruction. *Academic Therapy Quarterly, 4*(4), 277–282.

Hoffman, J. V., & Isaacs, M. E. (1991). Developing fluency through restructuring the task of guided oral reading. *Theory Into Practice, 30,* 185–194.

Horwitz, B., Rumsey, J. M., & Donahue, B. C. (1998, January 18). Functional connectivity of the angular gyrus in normal reading and dyslexia. *Proceedings of the National Academy of Sciences, USA, 95,* 8939–8944.

Hyerle, D. (2000). *A field guide to using visual tools.* Alexandria, VA: ASCD.

Johnson, D., & Pearson, P. (1984). *Teaching reading vocabulary* (2nd ed.). New York: Holt Reinhart & Winston.

Kagan, S. (1990). *Cooperative learning.* San Clemente, CA: Kagan Cooperative.

Kolb, D. (1984). *Experiential learning: Experience as the source of learning and development.* Englewood Cliffs, NJ: Prentice Hall.

Kuzmich, L. (1980). Neurophysiological development: A review for educators. *The Journal of Professional Studies, 5*(1), 26–34.

Kuzmich, L. (1987, Summer). *Supported mainstreaming of mild to moderately handicapped students.* Paper presented at the Northern Regional Conference for Special Education, University of Northern Colorado.

Kuzmich, L. (1998). *Data-driven instruction: A handbook.* Longmont, CO: Centennial Board of Cooperative Services.

Kuzmich, L. (2003, June). *Vocabulary acquisition.* Paper presented at the Professional Development Conference for High School Teachers in the New Orleans Archdiocese. Loveland, CO: KCS.

Levine, M. (1990). *Keeping a head in school.* Cambridge, MA: Educator's Publishing Service.

Levine, M. (2002). *A mind at a time.* New York: Simon & Schuster.

Loewen, J. (1995). *Lies my teacher told me: Everything your American history textbook got wrong.* New York: New York Press.

Logan, D. (2000). *Information skills toolkit: Collaborative integrated instruction for the middle grades.* Worthington, OH: Linsworth Publishing.

Lou, Y., Abrami, P. C., Spence, J. C., Paulsen, D., Chamber, B., & d'Apollonio, S. (1996). Within class grouping: A meta-analysis. *Journal of Educational Research, 75,* 69–77.

Mackey, M. (1990). Filling the gaps: The Baby Sitters Club, the series books, and the learning reader. *Language Arts, 67,* 484–489.

Manzo, A. (1998). Teaching for creative outcomes: Why we don't, how we all can. *Clearing House, 71*(5).

Manzo, A. (2003). Literacy crisis or Cambrian period: Theory, practice, and public policy implications, *Journal of Adolescent and Adult Literacy, 46,* 654–661.

Manzo, A., Barnhill, A., Land, A., Manzo, U., & Thomas, M. (1997). *Discovery of proficient reader subtypes: Implications for literacy theory and practices.* Paper presented at the College Reading Association Conference, Boston, MA.

Manzo, A., Manzo, U., & Albee, J. (2002). iREAP: Improving reading, writing, and thinking in the wired classroom. *Journal of Adolescent & Adult Literacy, 46,* 42–47.

Manzo, A., Manzo, U., Barnhill, A., & Thomas, M. (2000). Proficient reader subtypes: Implications for literacy theory, assessment, and practice. *Reading Psychology, 21,* 217–232.

Manzo, A., Manzo, U., & Estes, T. (2001). *Content area literacy: Interactive teaching for active learning* (3rd ed.). New York: John Wiley.

Marston, D., & Magnusseon, D. (1988). *Curriculum-based measurement: District level implementation.* Washington, DC: National Association of School Psychologists.

Martinez, M. G., Roser, N. L., & Strecker, S. (1999). I never thought I could be a star. A readers theatre ticket to fluency. *The Reading Teacher, 52,* 326–334.

Marzano, R. (2003). *What works in schools: Translating research into action.* Alexandria,VA: ASCD.

Marzano, R. (2004, January). *Making a difference: How school leaders can positively impact student achievement.* Paper presented at the Colorado Association of School Executives, Denver.

Marzano, R., & Arredondo, D. (1996). *Tactics for Thinking.* Alexandria, VA: ASCD.

Marzano, R., Norford, J., Paynter, D., Gaddy, B., & Pickering, D. (2001). *Handbook for classroom instruction that works.* Alexandria, VA: ASCD.

Marzano, R., Pickering, D., & Pollack, J. (2001). *Classroom instruction that works: Research-based strategies for increasing student achievement.* Aurora, CO: McREL.

McCarthy, B. (1990). Using the 4MAT system to bring learning styles to schools. *Education Leadership, 48*(2), 31–33.

McCarthy, B. (2000). *About teaching: 4MAT in the classroom.* Wanconda, FL: About Learning, Inc.

McCombs, B., & Whistler, S. (1997). *The learner-centered classroom and school: Strategies for increasing student motivation and achievement.* San Francisco: Jossey-Bass.

McCune, B. (2002). *Adjuncts for English language acquisition: Summary of research paper prepared for Colorado State Library English Language Acquisition Unit.* Retrieved on August 6, 2004, from http://www.cde.state.co.us/c-tag/download/pdf/ELA_ADJUNCTS.pdf

McEwan, E. (2002). *Teach them all to read: Catching the kids who fall through the cracks.* Thousand Oaks, CA: Corwin Press.

McGuinness, D. (1997). *Why our children can't read.* New York: Free Press.

McNeeley, C., Nonnemaker, J., & Blum, R. (2002). Promoting school connectedness: Evidence from the National Longitudinal Study of Adolescent Health. *The Journal of School Health, 72*(40), 138–146.

McTighe, J., & Lyman, F. (1988, April). Cueing thinking in the classroom: The promise of theory-embedded tools. *Educational Leadership, 45*(7), 7.

Mezynski, K. (1983). Issues concerning the acquisition of knowledge: Effects of vocabulary training on reading comprehension. *Review of Education Research, 53,* 253–279.

Miccinati, J. L. (1985). Using prosodic cues to teach oral reading fluency. *The Reading Teacher, 40,* 70–75.

Miller, R. (1990). *What are schools for? Holistic education in American culture.* Brandon, VT: Holistic Education Press.

Miller, S. (2003). Teachers as co-learners and advocates for diversity. *Thinking Classroom, 4*(3), 21–28.

Nagy, W. (2000). *Teaching vocabulary to improve reading comprehension.* (NCTE/ERIC: ISBN: 08141-5238-4, IRA ISBN: 087207-151-0, IRA No. 151)

Nathan, R. G., & Stanovich, K. E. (1991). The causes and consequences of differences in reading fluency. *Theory Into Practice, 30,* 176–184.

Neeld, E. C. (1986) *Writing* (2nd ed). Glenview, IL: Scott Foresman.

Newkirk, T. (2002). *Misreading masculinity: Boys, literacy and popular culture.* Portsmouth, NH: Heinemann.

Ogle, D. M. (1986). K-W-L: A teaching model that develops active reading of expository text. *The Reading Teacher, 39,* 564–570.

Ogle, D. M. (1989). The know, want to know, learn strategy. In K. D. Muth (Ed.), *Children's comprehension of text: Research into practice* (pp. 205–223). Newark, DE: International Reading Association.

O'Keefe, J., & Nadel, L. (1978). *The hippocampus as a cognitive map.* Oxford: Clarendon Press.

O'Neill, J. (1995). On preparing students for the world of work: A conversation with Willard Daggett. *Educational Leadership, 52*(8), 46–48.

Ornstein, R., & Sobel, D. (1987). *The healing brain.* New York: Simon & Schuster.

Ornstein, R., & Thompson, R. (1984). *The amazing brain.* Boston: Houghton Mifflin.

Panksepp, J. (1998). *Affective neuroscience: The foundations of human and animal emotions.* New York: Oxford University Press.

Parry, T., & Gregory, G. (2003). *Designing brain-compatible learning.* Arlington Heights, IL: Skylight Publishing and Training.

Pascopella, A. (2003). The next challenge. *District Administrator, 39,* 24–30.

Paul, R. & Elder, L. (2001). *Critical thinking tools for taking charge of your learning and your life.* Englewood Cliffs, NJ: Prentice Hall.

Paul, R., & Elder, L. (2002). *The art of asking essential questions.* San Francisco, CA: The Foundation for Critical Thinking.

Paul, R., & Elder, L. (2003). *The foundations of analytic thinking: How to take thinking apart and what to look for when you do.* San Francisco, CA: The Foundation for Critical Thinking.

Payne, R. (2001). *A framework for understanding poverty.* Highlands, TX: aha! Process.

Peterson, R., & Eeds, M. (1990). *Grand conversations: Literature groups in action.* New York: Scholastic.

Perkins, D. (1984). Creativity by design. *Educational Leadership, 42*(1), 18–24.

Pinnell, G., & Fountas, I. (1996). *Guided reading: Good first teaching for all children.* Portsmouth, NH: Heinemann.

RAND. (2002). Reading for understanding: Toward an R&D program. In *Reading comprehension.* Santa Monica, CA: Author.

Readence, E., & Moore, D. W. (Eds.). *Reading in the content areas* (2nd ed., pp. 229–234). Dubuque, IA: Kendall/Hunt.

Reeves, D. B. (2000). *Accountability in action: A blueprint for learning organizations.* Denver, CO: Advanced Learning Press and Center for Performance Assessment.

Reissman, R. (2001). Face forward. *Oasis, 17,* 54–57.

Richards, M. (2000). Be a good detective: Solve the case of oral reading fluency. *The Reading Teacher, 53*(7), 534–539.

Routman, R. (1991). *Invitations changing as teachers and learners K–12.* Portsmouth, NH: Heinemann.

Rowe, M. B. (1987). Wait time: Slowing down may be a way of speeding up. *Education, 11*(i), 43.

Ryan, J., & Capra, S. (2001). *Information literacy toolkit*. Chicago: American Library Association.

Sadker, D. (2002). An educator's primer on the gender war. *Phi Delta Kappan, 84,* 235–240.

Sagan, C. (1996). *The demon-haunted world: Science as a candle in the dark* (pp. 293–306). New York: Ballantine Books.

Schwartz, S., & Bone, M. (1995). *Retelling, relating, reflecting beyond the 3 r's*. Toronto, ON: Irwin Publishing.

Silver, H. F., Strong, R. W., & Perini, M. J. (2000). *So each may learn: Integrating learning styles and multiple intelligences*. Arlington, VA: ASCD.

Simkins, M., Cole, K., Tavalin, F., & Means, B. (2002). *Increasing student learning through multimedia projects*. Alexandria, VA: ASCD.

Simmons, R. (2001). *Odd girl speaks out: Girls write about bullies, cliques, popularity and jealousy*. Glenview, IL: Skylight Professional/Pearson Publications.

Smith, M., & Wilhelm, J. (2002). *Reading don't fix no Chevy's: Literacy in the lives of young men*. Portsmouth, NH: Heinemann.

Snow, C. E., Burns, M. S., & Griffin, P. (Eds.). (1998). *Preventing reading difficulties in young children*. Washington, DC: National Academy Press.

Sousa, D. (1995). *How the brain learns*. Reston, VA: National Association of Secondary School Principals.

Sousa, D. (2001). *How the brain learns* (2nd ed.). Thousand Oaks, CA: Corwin Press.

Sousa, D. (2003, December 6). *Helping teachers and learners design brain-compatible schools*. Presentation at National Staff Development Council Annual Conference, New Orleans, LA.

Springer, S., & Deutsch, G. (1985). *Left brain, right brain*. New York: W. H. Freeman and Company.

St. John, E. P., Loescher, S. A., & Bardzell, J. S. (2003). *Improving reading and literacy in grades 1–5: A resource guide to research-based programs*. Thousand Oaks, CA: Corwin Press.

Stahl, S., & Fairbanks, M. (1986). The effects of vocabulary instruction: A model-based meta-analysis. *Review of Educational Research, 56,* 72–110.

Stanovich, K. E. (1986). Matthew effects in reading: Some consequences of individual differences in the acquisition of literacy. *Reading Research Quarterly, 21,* 360–407.

Stasz, B., & Tankersley, D. (2003). Community as a source for literacy instruction. *The Thinking Classroom, 4,* 8–13.

Stayter, F. Z., & Allinton, R. L. (1991). *Fluency and the understanding of texts. Theory Into Practice, 30,* 143–148.

Sternberg, R. (1996). *Successful intelligence: How practical and creative intelligence determine success in life*. New York: Simon & Schuster.

Sternberg, R. (1998). Teaching and assessing for successful intelligence. *School Administrator, 55,* 26–31.

Stevenson, J., Howard, C., Coard, S., Wallace, S., & Brotman, L. (2004). Towards culturally relevant preventive interventions: The consideration of racial socialization in parent training with African American families. *Journal of Child and Family Studies, 13,* 277–294.

Strong, R., Silver, H., Perini, M., & Tuculescu, G. (2002). *Reading for academic success: Powerful strategies for struggling, average, and advanced readers, grades 7–12*. Thousand Oaks, CA: Corwin Press.

Sum, A., Kirsch, I., & Taggart, R. (2002, February). The twin challenges of mediocrity and inequality: Literacy in the U.S. from an international perspective. *Policy*

Information Report, Policy Information Center: Educational testing Service. Retrieved August 6, 2004, from http://www.ets.org/research/pic/twinchall.pdf

Sylwester, R. (1995). *A celebration of neurons: An educator's guide to the brain.* Alexandria, VA: ASCD.

Thornburg, D. (1991). *Education, technology, and paradigms of change for the 21st century.* Lake Barrington, IL: David Thornberg and Starsong Publications.

Tomlinson, C. (2001). How to differentiate instruction in mixed-ability classrooms (2nd ed.). Alexandria, VA: ASCD.

Tompkins, G. E. (1998). *50 literacy strategies step by step.* Upper Saddle River, NJ: Merrill/Prentice Hall.

Tompkins, G. (2003). *Literacy for the 21st century* (3rd ed.). Columbus, OH: Merrill/Prentice Hall.

Torrance, E. P. (1998). *Why fly? A philosophy of creativity.* Norwood, NJ: Ablex Publishing Corporation.

Tovani, C. (2000). *I read it, but I don't get it.* Portland, MD: Stenhouse Publisher.

U.S. Department of Health and Human Services: National Institutes of Health. (2000). *Report of the National Reading Panel: Teaching children to read reports of subgroups* (NIH Publication No. 00-4754). Washington, DC: Author.

U.S. Secretary of Labor. (1991). *What work requires of schools: A SCANS report for America 2000.* The Secretary's Commission on Achieving Necessary Skills (SCANS). Washington, DC: U.S. Department of Labor.

Vacca, R., & Vacca, J. (2002). *Content area reading: Literacy and learning across the curriculum.* Boston, MA: Allyn & Bacon.

Van Strien, J. W., Stolk, B. D., & Zuiker, S. (1995). Hemisphere-specific treatment of dyslexia subtypes: Better reading with anxiety-laden words? *Journal of Learning Disabilities, 28*(1), 30–34.

Watts-Taffe, S., Gwinn, C., Johnson, J., & Horn, M. (2003). Preparing pre-service teachers to integrate technology with the elementary literacy program. *The Reading Teacher, 57,* 130–138.

Whitehead, A. (1967). *Aims of education and other essays* (Rev. ed.). New York: Free Press. (Original work published 1929)

Wolfe, P. (2001). *Brain matters: Translating research into classroom practice.* Alexandria, VA: Association for Supervision and Curriculum Development.

Wolfe, P., & Brandt, R. (1998). What do we know from brain research? *Educational Leadership, 56*(3), 8–13.

Wood, C. (1994). *Yardsticks, children in the classroom.* Greenfield, MA: Northeast Foundation for Children.

Zutell, J., & Rasinski, T. V. (1991). Training teachers to attend to their students' oral reading fluency. *Theory Into Practice, 30,* 211–217.

Index

**CORWIN
PRESS**

The Corwin Press logo—a raven striding across an open book—represents the union of courage and learning. Corwin Press is committed to improving education for all learners by publishing books and other professional development resources for those serving the field of K–12 education. By providing practical, hands-on materials, Corwin Press continues to carry out the promise of its motto: **"Helping Educators Do Their Work Better."**